CINCINNATI AND
SOUTHWEST OHIO'S
HAUNTED MEMORIES

CINCINNATI AND SOUTHWEST OHIO'S HAUNTED MEMORIES

Jeff Morris and Michael A. Morris

ARCADIA
PUBLISHING

Published by Arcadia Publishing
Charleston, South Carolina

Printed in the United States of America

Library of Congress Control Number: 2009920478

For all general information contact Arcadia Publishing at:
Telephone 843-853-2070
Fax 843-853-0044
E-mail sales@arcadiapublishing.com
For customer service and orders:
Toll-Free 1-888-313-2665

Visit us on the Internet at www.arcadiapublishing.com

Contents

ACKNOWLEDGMENTS

The images in this book come from the authors' collection, unless otherwise noted. Other images were courtesy of many different people and organizations: the Dan Finfrock collection, Delhi Historical Society, Whitewater Township Historical Society, Cincinnati Historical Society, Mount Healthy Historical Society, Indian Hill Historical Society, the Knights of the Golden Trail, Cincinnati Area Paranormal Existence Research (CAPER), and the Butler County Historical Society.

Many other people and organizations were kind enough to share their knowledge of both history and hauntings at many of the locations mentioned in this book: Liberty Township Historical Society, Hamilton County Public Libraries, Hamilton County Sheriff's Department, Price Hill Historical Society, Whitewater Township Historical Society, Delhi Historical Society, Butler County Historical Society, Mount Healthy Historical Society, Indian Hill Historical Society, Cincinnati Historical Society, Colerain Historical Society, and the staff at the Cincinnati Art Museum, Music Hall, Habits Café, 20th Century Theater, Taft Museum of Art, Loveland Castle, and Hamilton County Parks.

Also, thank you to Fr. Jim Meade, George Korns, Larry Shab, Diane Bauchman, Harvey Crihfield, Rebecca Hosta, Peg Schmidt, Joan Hendricks, Sgt. Ron Reckers, Caroline Huppi, Jim Rahtz, Joy Landry, Scott Santangelo, Beth Gilley, Michael Riesenberg, Diane Ward, Mike Kidd, Dick Scheid, Mark Rogers, Aaron Rokoe, Patrick Brande, Linda J. Bailey, Dan Finfrock, and Sir Fred and the other Knights of the Golden Trail.

Without the information and photographs that we were able to obtain from all of you, this book would never have come to be. You have our most sincere thank-you.

A special thank-you to Melissa Basilone and John Pearson with Arcadia Publishing, without them this book would still only be an idea. They have been very patient and understanding.

Finally, we extend a well-deserved thank-you to our wives, children, and parents. Without their support and understanding we would not have had the time to compile this book.

We can never thank you enough.

FOREWORD

How do you believe in something that you have never seen? Is hearing enough to prove something is real? Should I just believe in it because someone told me it was real? When does one know the truth? When is the evidence solid enough to render you speechless?

I am an avid paranormal enthusiast. Not only do I enjoy the Hollywood reenactments of far-fetched, unrealistic hauntings, but I also enjoy walking through a reputedly haunted building or driving a haunted street multiple times after dark. This fascination with the paranormal sat idle most of my life. I never truly thought about it until about five years ago, after I met my wife and moved back to Cincinnati from New Jersey.

Once I settled back into Cincinnati, where I was born and raised, Jeff and I began doing our own investigations. We would travel to the small haunted locations we read about online that we were legally allowed to enter after dark. Once we got there, we would take pictures with our digital cameras and let our digital recorder run. We would stay for about an hour only hearing the cars passing and the crickets chirping, only seeing the trees and brush that surrounded us. Then we would leave with nothing but the hope that we had captured something on one of our electronic devices.

After getting home and reviewing the evidence, we would usually come up with nothing. This lack of fulfilling evidence, however, did not deter me from trying again. We would repeat this when we could and eventually came home with something unusual. Sometimes we would get an orb that seemed too large or too round to explain away as lens flare or a bug. Sometimes we would hear voices on our recorder that we did not recall being there.

But, much to my disappointment, we never saw a ghost. This is not to say I do not believe they exist. I believe I can say I have heard a ghost and that was enough to change me from a confused skeptic to a believer. We captured things that could not be explained away with a reasonable, logical, scientific explanation. When we tried to give the explanation, it became so far-fetched and exaggerated it seemed nearly impossible.

As we continued these investigations and our interests grew, we decided to find out more. We had heard from the legends that brutal murders, horrific fires, and tragic events had occurred at these locations. We began to wonder if these murders and tragedies actually did ever happen, so we began our search for the truth.

At the time, we both worked downtown as instructors at a local college, and between every class, at every lunch, and at every break, we would walk a couple blocks down the road to the Hamilton County Library main branch. The library expanded over two city blocks with three floors. We did not know where to begin when all we had to go on was a street name. We continued to search for historical truths to the ghost stories for the majority of the year. Every step we took brought us a little closer to finding something bigger. We would talk to someone who would give us another name of someone who might know more. Eventually, we would have a date and a name to go along with the reported legend. In the end, the legend that spoke of a brutal murder became the history of a real brutal murder occurring at the very spot it was supposed to have happened.

During this research and the writing of the book, we realized that Cincinnati's ghosts were not often talked about. Southwestern Ohio had no year-round walking ghost tours, only a guided bus tour that runs once a year. After attending several tours in Tennessee and Pennsylvania, we decided Cincinnati needed a year-round walking tour. However, we knew downtown Cincinnati would be too large and not a safe place to walk around at night. So we chose a small town 20 minutes from downtown known as Miamitown. After a couple months of talking to residents, historians, store owners, and the historical society, we finally started Miamitown Ghost Tours in December 2006.

Our hard work and research was not put to sleep. The various locations we had studied and researched came together into this book. Before long, we had over five historical societies, the local sheriff's department, the management of many of the tourist attractions, and several locals telling us more information and giving us the opportunity to include their photographs. This book would not be in your hands today without these people. Library books and newspaper articles can tell you the facts, but the words of an eyewitness can say so much more. Without them, we would have ended this book before it ever truly started.

In the end, I have determined that every spirit that walks this earth walks this earth for a reason. Some because they died too soon and wanted to finish off what they had begun; some because they were angry with someone or something; and others to just remain in the place that they once loved or to be near those that they loved. If spirits exist, they exist with a purpose and a goal.

Michael A. Morris
September 22, 2008

INTRODUCTION

I saw a ghost once, although I do not believe in them. I call it my ghost paradox. How do I explain it then? I try not to because it always tends to happen that my explanations (a trick of the light, an overzealous prankster breaking and entering after hours) ring less true than the possibility that something unnatural happened—at least in the eyes of those to whom I tell the story. I wonder if that is a quirk of human nature—to always strive to believe the more fanciful explanation. Although in my own mind, I cannot bring myself to accept the existence of ghosts, I find myself constantly pursuing the stories and the legends. I find myself constantly hoping that I am wrong and that the legends are more than just urban myths. My ghost lives in a movie theater.

The Showcase Cinemas in Western Hills is supposedly haunted. The stories about it are not widespread though. The stories are only personal experiences spread among management and employees. Anyone who knows the stories has worked there or known someone who has worked there. While the theater bustles during business hours and runs business as normal most of the time, its silence echoes as soon as the patrons have left. Those employees who remain there after hours to close the business day and to prepare for the next are the ones who experience the place's chilling personality.

When I was first introduced to the stories of this haunted theater, I worked there as a manager. As I was working on closing the day, I was told some of the stories of people who have seen weird things within those walls. Once a manager had been watching a film by herself after hours, supposedly the only one in the 14-screen multiplex. She heard a sound behind her and glanced back to see someone sitting several rows behind her, watching the film with her. She fled in terror and telephoned the police. No one was in the building. As a result of this occurrence, policy within the theater changed. No one, not even managers, are allowed in the building alone after hours.

Another story focuses on the ceiling tiles that rest two stories above the patrons' seats. No matter how often they are replaced, they will pop out during the night. The building has no ladder that will reach that high, not even the cherry picker with which banners are hung in the lobby. The only thing that the building has that can reach that height is scaffolding that takes the efforts of several people to construct. Still, something manages to pop out those tiles regularly. All these stories focus around screen 10, down the right hallway, last door on the left. The staff calls it the haunted theater.

I always enjoyed hearing these stories while I worked there. The extra little buzz of excitement that I would get while nearing screen 10 would make the day move a little bit faster. I never believed that the theater was actually haunted though. Ill-fitting tiles and people sneaking into the theater after hours through an overlooked, unlocked door seemed more logical explanations to me. But despite knowing that there is no such thing as ghosts, closing down the dark projector for screen 10 and checking the back exit door would always send chills down my spine. The stories themselves were almost causing the "ghosts" to come alive.

I saw my ghost at 3:00 in the morning on a Tuesday.

I was managing a maintenance shift with three teenage employees that night. The purpose of the shift was to change burned-out lightbulbs throughout the building. These bulbs had to be changed after hours because it would take a lot of time to build the scaffolding necessary to reach them. So the shift started at midnight as the last customers were leaving the building and the staff was closing down the business day.

Most of the shift was uneventful. The employees and I were constantly together, and the creepiness of the theater fails to show itself when there are others around. We moved quickly and efficiently, knowing that we would be paid for the entire shift even if we were to finish and leave earlier than scheduled. So as the shift neared its end, we began putting away the scaffolding down the east hallway.

The theater itself is shaped like a Y. The lobby, customer service, and the concession stand form the base of the Y while two hallways with seven screens apiece angle away from it. Screen 10 sits at the end of the right hallway. That hallway was where we were putting away the scaffolding.

As we were finishing for the day, out of the corner of my eye I saw a figure cross the lobby and disappear around the corner into the other hallway. In all honesty, at the time I did not think a whole lot of it. I only barely saw it out of the corner of my eye and figured it was a trick of the light on the front windows or a hallucination caused from the late hour and lack of sleep. That is, I did not think much of it until one of the other employees asked me if I had seen it.

A chill went down my spine as I asked him what he had seen. He explained to me in detail the figure that I had seen out of the corner of my eye. Of course, the first thought that entered my mind was that someone had wandered into the theater after hours through an unlocked door, so the employees and I walked cautiously down into the lobby to check. We found all the doors secure but figured that the door could have secured behind the unauthorized visitor. We then proceeded to check the screens down the hallway where we saw the figure walk.

After another hour of fruitlessly searching the building, we decided that it was empty. We checked the angle of the front windows to see if what we saw was just a reflection of us putting away the scaffolding. It could not have been. The windows reflected off to the right too far. We were stuck in a building with a figure that two of us had seen and no explanation for whom or what it could have been.

We left the building soon after that, hoping that if someone had snuck into the theater and hidden from us, they would trigger the alarms that I set before I left. The alarms never went off that night. I was stuck having seen a "ghost" and yet not believing in them. I was stuck with my ghost paradox.

Over the next few days, we all told our story to the other employees. They met the story with the same skepticism with which I had met the stories that I had heard previously. I did not really believe that I had seen a ghost myself, but despite this I still enjoyed telling everyone the story.

I have since left the theater. I have not even been back there in a while. I have heard from friends that I still have there that most everyone who was there when I was has left. I have often been curious to go back there sometime when there are all new faces there to ask if anyone had heard the old ghost stories about the place. I have not yet asked because I have got this hope in the back of my head that one day I will go back there and hear my own story recounted to me. I want to hear my own ghost story carried on from staff to staff through oral tradition. It would feel more important.

That was my inspiration for this book. While I do not know and will probably never know whether ghosts actually exist, I know that it is the stories that keep people interested in it. Through this book, I hope to help carry these stories from around Cincinnati through the ages in a more permanent way than simple oral tradition will. Putting the stories and the history behind them in print will do more to carry these from generation to generation. While I hope to one day hear my own story recalled by someone else, I hope I can give someone else that same satisfaction.

Showcase Cinemas Western Hills has never had a fatality on the premises. I looked into it and found that to be true. The area was nothing but a farmhouse with a picnic shelter before it was a theater, not a cemetery or an asylum. Despite being built as recently as 1994, it could be shut down soon. The ground that it was built on is sliding down a hill, and one day the theater itself will follow. Remarkably, the first part of the building that will crumble and fall off the hill is screen 10.

In creating this book, my brother and I have come across many ghost stories from in and around Cincinnati. While some of the ghosts that we have heard about are securely anchored in historical tragedy, there were also some ghosts that seemed to have no historical source. While the ghosts that had historical backstories were more interesting and take up the bulk of this book, there were at least a couple of fun stories that seemed more like urban myths.

We heard about a stretch of road just outside of Colerain Township through which an especially dangerous ghost supposedly roams.

Not too far from Lick Road, there resides one of the more unusual ghosts of southwestern Ohio. One would not even guess that this road was haunted, looking at it from its genesis at Pippin Road. Buell Road extends to the west at Triple Creek Park through a well-lit, pleasant area of Hamilton County. Soon, though, the lights of the park are swallowed by the thick, surrounding woods, and the road itself becomes bathed in darkness.

Buell Road twists and turns through these trees before suddenly straightening up for one long stretch of asphalt. The road curves and climbs constantly except for this section. This area of the road, punctuated only by a rusted guardrail and a fire hydrant, is where the ghost of Buell rides at night.

Legends say that there are a couple of things to keep in mind when approaching this spirit.

First, one has to summon the spirit. To do this, one must flash his or her headlights three times. Off then on. Off then on. Off then on. Then off again. At this point you sit and wait. When the ghost appears, it will take the form of a little boy on a bicycle, which approaches suddenly from the corner behind you. If you have your windows down, it is said that you can even hear the vibrations of the bicycle's spokes as it approaches.

This brings you to the second thing to keep in mind when approaching this spirit. The legend goes on to say that if the boy on the bicycle reaches you before you turn back on your lights, you will die in seven days.

Of course, this was a legend that we thought would be fun to test out. We drove down Buell Road until we reached the haunted section and stopped the car. Despite not really believing this legend at all, the clichéd chills crawled almost painfully down our spines as we prepared to flash our lights.

Off then on.

Was that a bicycle reflector up ahead or just the curious eyes of a cautious raccoon?

Off then on.

Nothing, just the darkness of the road suggesting the impossibility of seeing anything, even our ghost, in the pitch of the night.

Off then on.

Then off again.

Were the crickets singing in the woods? Even if they were, would a bicycle sound any different?

In the daylight, urban myths can seem almost comical, almost transparently playing upon certain human fears like a bad morality tale. In the daylight, one can ask questions like, "What do flashing headlights have to do with this boy on the bike?" or "How does one die after seven days exactly?" In the daylight, this stretch of road takes on an environmental beauty, the greens and browns of the trees filling nature's breathtaking canvas.

But at night, the ridiculousness of the myth gets lost somewhere along the way. At night, those logical questions that one might ask seem inconsequential.

At night, there is no beauty, only fear.

—Jeff Morris

One

NORTHWEST CINCINNATI

There is a place, not too far from anywhere, where the mood and atmosphere of the place can alone create ghosts. Perhaps the ambiance of this place, the lights from civilization swallowed by the skeletal trees of this secluded road, the grainy quality of those piercing horror films echoed in the post-twilight mist of the creek, haunt these forsaken places.

From Mount Pleasant to Pleasant Avenue: Quarantine

In 1849, something terrible happened in Cincinnati. First, people would start getting terrible cramps in their abdomen. They would double over in pain. They would have debilitating diarrhea and would begin to vomit uncontrollably. Only a couple hours after the first symptoms struck the unfortunate victims, they would die.

It was called cholera, and it was a terrible way to die. In 1849, an epidemic unlike any that Cincinnati had ever seen suddenly swept into the city and infected thousands. Apparently, sanitation practices throughout the city were poor at best. Sewage and human waste were somehow becoming mixed up with drinking water and food supplies in the city. As more and more people began to become infected, panic began to roll through the city.

Up until this point in history, Ohio had almost been immune to deadly outbreaks of disease. Almost 20 years earlier in 1832, a small outbreak of cholera had erupted in Cleveland, likely spread from European trade across Lake Erie. Cincinnati, though, had barely any experience with the disease.

As the 1840s were coming to a close, the Ohio River was carrying a lot of trade and supplies from the east to Cincinnati. Somehow the poor sanitary conditions of the big city, coupled with the cholera germs transferred from the east, caused an outbreak in the city.

The results were terrible. Somewhere between 10,000 and 20,000 people in Cincinnati became infected with the disease. The mortality rate of those infected was brutal. Somewhere between 40 and 80 percent of those infected would die from the disease only hours after they first exhibited any symptoms.

Since the doctors in the city did not have any idea what caused the disease or how to cure it, the treatments for the disease were often as bad as the disease itself. One such treatment was the prescription of the drug calomel. Calomel often killed those who took it faster than the disease itself could. The drug contained mercury, which is a highly poisonous element. Mercury poisoning was almost as painful as cholera itself.

The people of Cincinnati were afraid. They knew that they had to find some way to escape.

Just north of Cincinnati, there was a little village known as Mount Pleasant. Mount Pleasant grew around the intersection of two Native American trails that passed through the area about halfway between Fort Washington in Cincinnati and Fort Hamilton in what is today Hamilton. The area was plotted in the early 1800s. Partially thanks to newspaper articles encouraging people from the city to move to the area, the square mile that was set up as Mount Pleasant was quickly settled.

Mount Pleasant grew like many other towns in the area in the 1800s. Hamilton Avenue, or Main Street as it was called in the 1800s, moved through the area, eventually stretching as far north as Hamilton and as far south as Cincinnati. All along this road, passing wagons and horses would be charged tolls every two miles for use of the road. In 1980, one of those tollbooths that sat on Hamilton Avenue was physically moved to Mount Healthy Park and is currently used as a piece of the Mount Healthy Museum.

In the early 1820s, there were still no established churches in the area, so local preachers would hold services in private residences throughout the town. Eventually the town grew too much for the small homes in the area to accommodate such large crowds, and the town decided to construct a free meetinghouse where these preachers could hold their sermons. In 1825, the Free Meeting House in Mount Pleasant was constructed.

Anyone who wanted to use the building was welcome to it. It was used on a first-come-first-served basis, and whenever there was any question of who was going to use the house on any particular day, the competing parties would roll dice to determine who would use it that day.

Eventually, churches were built in the area, but the Free Meeting House continued to be used. Civic meetings were often held in the building. The police and fire departments were once housed within its walls. At one point, there was a one-cell jail in the building.

In 1963, this building was also moved to Mount Healthy Park, where it currently houses the Mount Healthy Historical Society Museum.

Mount Pleasant continued to grow and flourish until 1849, when the cholera epidemic struck Cincinnati. While much of the Cincinnati area was under siege from the epidemic, Mount Pleasant was able to somehow continue to remain healthy. The disease would ultimately kill more than 8,000 people in the city of Cincinnati (including Harriet Beecher Stowe's son), but there were no deaths from cholera in the village of Mount Pleasant.

Mount Pleasant began to gain the reputation in the area as a place that was immune to the disease. People from Cincinnati who wanted to save themselves and their families from the epidemic decided that they would move north to the village of Mount Pleasant.

While residents of Mount Pleasant were proud that they had been able to avoid the epidemic up to this point, they did not have the feeling that they were completely immune to the disease. They feared that the influx of people coming into the town from infected Cincinnati would cause an outbreak of cholera in their town.

Some historians believe that at this point, Mount Pleasant residents took drastic measures to assure their own health. In 1849 and 1850, Mount Pleasant residents decided that they would quarantine their town. They would stop all outsiders from entering from any of the roads that led into town. When the trains would attempt to stop in Mount Pleasant to unload, the people of the town would force the train to move on without unloading anything.

The people from Cincinnati were scared and trying to flee to this safe haven of Mount Pleasant, but Mount Pleasant was scared of the outsiders and the germs that they might be carrying.

Until the cholera epidemic ended in 1850, Mount Pleasant secluded itself from the rest of the area. Soon after the cholera epidemic ended and Mount Pleasant began opening its doors to new settlers, the U.S. post office notified them that there was another town in Ohio with the name of Mount Pleasant and that they had to change their name. The citizens of Mount Pleasant were unanimous in deciding that the new name of their town should be Mount Healthy in honor of their health throughout the cholera epidemic of 1849 and 1850.

There are many people who say that many of the ghosts that plague Mount Healthy to this day are somehow remnants of what had happened in the middle of the 1800s.

Mount Healthy is now a part of the Greater Cincinnati area. It is within the I-275 bypass loop, and while it is officially a city of its own, everyone from around the area considers it a neighborhood of Cincinnati. Many roads and highways move through Mount Healthy, and the need for train tracks ended long ago. Tracks had once passed through the western edge of town near the Arlington Memorial Gardens cemetery, but they have long since vanished.

In 1825, the Free Meeting House was built on Hamilton Avenue in order to accommodate large crowds for civic meetings and church sermons. Eventually, this building housed the police and fire department headquarters. At one point, it even held a single-celled jail. As the town's population grew and churches were built, the Free Meeting House was no longer needed for certain events; however, it would still be used for civic meetings on a first-come-first-served basis. If more than one group wanted to use the house on the same day, a roll of the dice would determine who got to use the building. This photograph shows the Free Meeting House being moved in 1963 from its location on Hamilton Avenue to McMakin Avenue within Mount Healthy Park, where it sits today. It sits next door to an old tollhouse that was also moved from Hamilton Avenue. Both of these buildings now house the Mount Healthy Historical Society and Museum. (Courtesy of the Mount Healthy Historical Society.)

This 1859 tollhouse was one of many that were placed along the Cincinnati and Hamilton Turnpike, a road that is today Hamilton Avenue. Any use of the road required payment of a toll, which varied depending upon what kind of vehicle one was using. A horse and rider would cost 3¢, while a four-wheeled vehicle being pulled by a horse or ox would cost 18.75¢. When the turnpike went out of business, the tollbooths continued to stand along the road for many years. Wesley Werner Post 513 of the American Legion owned this particular booth throughout the mid-1900s. In the 1970s, when it became obvious to the Mount Healthy Historical Society that this building was going to be destroyed, members asked the American Legion to donate the building to the historical society. The legion ended up selling the building to the historical society for $1 in 1979. It was then moved next to the Free Meeting House on McMakin Avenue. Today it is part of the haunted Mount Healthy Historical Society Museum. (Courtesy of the Mount Healthy Historical Society.)

Despite the lack of train tracks moving through Mount Healthy, many people will often hear train whistles echoing throughout the town. This occurs especially in the alleyways between buildings. Although there is no train and no earthly reason for anyone there to hear train whistles, these sourceless whistles are heard often throughout the town.

Locals say that the ghostly train whistle is a result of the cholera epidemic in 1849. They claim that the whistle is a remnant of those terrified people who attempted to flee to Mount Pleasant on the trains but were not allowed to set foot on the healthy soil. Some say that the whistles are echoes of these trains, constantly moving throughout the town, trying to find a place where they can stop and enter the paradise of Mount Pleasant.

These ghostly whistles might claim their origin from another possible historical source. Somewhere between 1913 and 1915, a terrible train accident occurred on these tracks on the western edge of Mount Healthy. Something happened that caused a train to suddenly derail in the Mount Healthy area. Perhaps the spirits of the victims of this accident are the reason for the ghostly train whistle that echoes throughout the haunted town.

The other hauntings throughout the town are more difficult to pin down with exact historic reasons. The Free Meeting House and Mount Healthy Park are reputed to be haunted. In both places, people will sometimes feel a chill down their spine and get the feeling that they are being watched. Sometimes people will even see shadowy figures that disappear into the dark corners of the building or into the distance at the park. Reports of these hauntings are so widespread that in 2004, a local paranormal investigative group actually went into the Free Meeting House and searched it for evidence of ghosts. Despite not coming up with any concrete evidence that there are ghosts within the building, the group did report feeling uncomfortable at times and seeing things out of the corner of their eyes during the investigation.

Perhaps the most haunted building in Mount Healthy, though, is the Grace E. Hunt School on the corner of Harrison Avenue and Compton Street.

The school building that stands at the site today was the second school to be built there. The first school was only a single floor with four rooms in the building and was built in the 1860s. Eventually more rooms were added to the building, and it became an eight-room high school in 1893.

The haunted school building that stands there today, the Grace E. Hunt building, was not constructed until 1910. It was named after one of the more famous and experienced schoolteachers from the area. Grace E. Hunt taught in Mount Healthy area schools for most of her life. Not only did she teach for 40 years, she also was married to one of the leaders of the Mount Healthy educational system, Charles A. Hunt.

Often people have reported feeling uncomfortable when inside the school building after the sun has gone down. Beyond this, many strange things seem to happen quite often at this building. The most common occurrence at the Grace E. Hunt School is that the lights will flicker at night. Many times the building will be closed for the night and the lights will be off throughout the building when suddenly they will begin to flicker on and off. Sometimes custodians in the building will witness this phenomenon, and sometimes passing motorists or pedestrians will notice that the lights in the windows at the school are flashing on and off well after closing.

Other stories that come out of the school involve the chalkboards in many of the classrooms. Many times, people will leave for the night and then come back in the morning to see that there are strange messages and drawings all over the chalkboard. Usually actual messages cannot be interpreted on these chalkboards; it just looks like scribbling all over the board. Every once in a while though, there is a decipherable message in chalk on the boards, despite the building being empty all night and no one having an opportunity to write it on the board. Messages such as "help me" or "get out" have been reported to have mysteriously appeared on the chalkboards. Also, other less clichéd ghostly messages have appeared upon the boards in the school.

Once a teacher walked into her classroom in the morning after there had been no one there all throughout the night, and she saw that there was something written on the board that was not there the night before. The board said "Homework for tomorrow" and it listed a group of assignments that had nothing to do with the classes that the teacher who first saw the message taught. She had not written the homework message on the board, and she could not imagine who could have possibly done it. No other classes took place in the room. She could only guess that a ghost had haunted her classroom during the night and had assigned homework as part of her midnight lesson.

If one were to follow Hamilton Avenue north from Mount Healthy, it changes its name near Butler County to Pleasant Avenue. This is in honor of Mount Healthy from the days when it was still Mount Pleasant.

Beth Israel Cemetery is a Jewish Cemetery on Pleasant Avenue. It sits nestled in a very urban area of town. Pleasant Avenue is constantly busy, even in the middle of the night. A hardware store, a pet store, and gas stations are all closely situated to the cemetery. In fact, the cemetery shares a metal fence with the parking lot of the hardware store next door.

Beth Israel itself is small as cemeteries go. One can easily see across its flat landscape, from one corner to the other. It is also kept up quite well. Despite some of the tombstones being 150 years old, they all look relatively new. The grass is kempt. The atmosphere is tranquil.

While traffic is constantly passing in front of the large metal gates, it is still quiet; a sense of serenity still envelops the place. One can hear his or her own footsteps echo regardless of how much activity is bustling outside the fence.

Beth Israel Cemetery is one of a series of Jewish cemeteries that were built in the Cincinnati area in the late 1800s. Many years earlier, in 1821, a man named Benjamin Lieb was dying and begged his friends to bury him as a Jew. Two of his friends bought a small tract of land to use as a graveyard and founded the first Jewish cemetery west of the Appalachian Mountains. It was named the Old Jewish Cemetery and was placed just west of downtown Cincinnati. At first there was not much need for the Jewish cemetery in town. In 1821, there were only six Jews in the entire city of Cincinnati.

By 1849, though, when the cholera epidemic hit, the Jewish community had grown in Cincinnati so much that Old Jewish Cemetery almost immediately filled to capacity. The Jewish community in Cincinnati and the surrounding areas had to build new Jewish cemeteries around the area to satisfy the growing Jewish population in the city. Beth Israel was ultimately a result of this need to expand the number of Jewish cemeteries around the area.

The haunting of this cemetery is quite different from many of the hauntings that are in this book. There are no reports of people seeing figures. There are no accounts of people seeing any strange lights or feeling any strange chill or hand on their shoulder. In fact, we came across no accounts of anyone hearing any strange sounds or voices while they walked through this cemetery.

This cemetery is a hotbed for EVP activity though. EVP stands for electronic voice phenomenon. What happens is that an audio recording is made, and while those making the recording hear nothing out of the ordinary, strange sourceless voices will say something onto the recording upon playback.

People making audio recordings at Beth Israel have often encountered this strange occurrence. They have heard everything from the clichéd "Help me" or "Get out" to less common voices like the laughter of children or the barking of dogs that were not there while recording.

Perhaps the wind through the trees or the cars passing on Pleasant Avenue have something to do with what comes up on the recordings. By induction, one can almost discredit any recordings taken here for this reason—a trick of acoustics, the passing cars or gentle wind singing as they pass across some surface.

Sometime between 1913 and 1915 on the western edge of Mount Healthy, locals watched in horror as a train came off the tracks and crashed into a ditch on the side of the road. Locals rushed to the accident in an attempt to save the helpless victims trapped inside but were unable to save them all. Several people died in this tragic accident. The cause of the derailment is unknown; however, people say that the spirits of those lost in the accident remain in Mount Healthy to this day. Some report the sounds of train whistles and the rumbles of trains where no tracks currently lie. Perhaps these sounds are the spirits of those who tried to come into the only healthy town in Cincinnati to avoid the cholera epidemic, angry that they were turned away at the train station. (Courtesy of the Mount Healthy Historical Society.)

Reported to be the most haunted building in Mount Healthy, the Grace E. Hunt School sits on the corner of Harrison Avenue and Compton Street. The Grace E. Hunt School was constructed in 1910 after the town outgrew the original eight-room high school. Grace E. Hunt was one of the more famous and experienced teachers from the area. She taught in Mount Healthy for over 40 years and was married to Charles A. Hunt, the leader of the Mount Healthy educational system. People report lights flickering on and off in the building when no one should be inside. Custodians report this occurring while they are there after hours; passing cars will see the phenomenon as well. Chalkboards that were wiped clean the previous day will have assignments or threatening messages written on them when teachers arrive for class. (Courtesy of the Mount Healthy Historical Society.)

But what if it is not a trick of the atmosphere? What if these people who rest here for eternity are trying to tell us one last thing so that they can finally rest in peace?

The Handlebar Ranch: Tiny Town

Street signs echo the stories that come from this secluded section of Colerain Township. Graffiti adorns three consecutive one-word signs whose original intent was to warn of sharp turns in the road ahead. They say, "Leave This Place."

A small village once sat nestled in the forest on a hillside just off Bank Road. The words *Handlebar Ranch* were etched into a wooden sign that hung over the entrance to the village.

The buildings were all made of wood and seemed somewhat dark and neglected. Pictures, painted with brightly colored acrylics, decorated many of the walls of this unique little town. A pickup truck with a trailer attached was decorated as if it had once been a part of a circus. But then rust began creeping into the wheel wells, and spiderwebs helped to couple the trailer to the bed of the truck.

The most unusual thing about the town is that everything in it seemed too small. The doors would only come up to a normal man's chest. Even the roofs of the town are no taller than an ordinary person.

The entire village seems quite surreal. There is something markedly eerie about the bright circus colors being overtaken by decay and spiders. There is something that is not quite right about the unusually small domiciles.

Legends say that the Handlebar Ranch was a retirement community for circus sideshow little people who wanted to escape the tormenting stares of the public. A group of little people gathered together and reportedly retreated to the seclusion of the forests of northern Colerain Township in an attempt to escape the life that they had known in the traveling circus.

While over the last few years the town looked decrepit and abandoned, some locals claim that this is still a community of little people attempting to hide from the public eye. People, even recently, have told accounts of approaching this secluded town and being chased away by its residents. Apparently, these gawkers are assaulted by little people yelling and throwing rocks at the unsuspecting cars.

More recently, things got worse for the residents of this small town. Local teenagers had heard the stories of people being chased away by little people, so they often decided to test out the rumors for themselves. The rumor was that if you ran into the middle of the town in the middle of the night and rang the bell that sat nestled under a central overhang, the little people would come out in droves, hurling rocks and firing BB guns at the intruders. Teenagers would ring the bell often at night to prove to their friends that they were brave enough to do so.

The legends say that these people have attempted to hide from the world. Those ominous signs and stories of the vengeful residents do something to keep those unwanted visitors away.

While this strange and tragic story is quite an interesting tale, it has little basis in fact. These stories of retired circus performers are nothing more than a local urban myth that was generated by the tiny buildings in the seemingly out-of-place abandoned little town.

Handlebar Ranch was not a town built by little people in the circus but was actually a business that operated during the 1970s. Percy and Anna Ritter decided to create an attraction near their Colerain Township home for the small children from the surrounding areas. It was a little pioneer ranch where all the buildings were child size, allowing those visiting children to feel that they were somehow a part of this fantasy village.

The main attraction at the ranch was the hayride. The Ritters had built five wagons especially for this hayride. Each of the five wagons had the capacity to hold up to 50 children at one time. A horse would carry the wagon around the grounds of the ranch.

Tiny Town, Munchkinland, or Handlebar Ranch? The locals know it by all three names. The reputation of the small town has gotten out of hand over the years. Handlebar Ranch was the name given to this abnormal town by Percy and Anna Ritter. Their intention for the town was to provide local children a day of fun. It was a small hayride where horses would carry visitors in a wagon around the town. The business thrived until the insurance costs brought the Ritters to the point where they needed to shut it down. The abandoned hayride quickly gained a reputation as a village of retired circus little people. Teenagers and locals continued to visit the small town at night to vandalize it and ring the small bell that sits at the town's center. This would wake the Ritters and their neighbors who had homes nearby. The small town was torn down in 2008.

Anna Ritter was also an artist, and she spent many hours meticulously decorating the little town. It was a unique project for her, being able to utilize her artistic skills in such a surreal environment. It was like she was painting the little town up to be a little miniature circus. She used bright colors and created interesting designs that she felt were certain to catch a child's eye.

Handlebar Ranch immediately became incredibly successful for its owners, and it became a favorite recreational destination in Colerain Township during the 1970s.

Every chance that the Ritters got, they would add little trinkets and accessories to the miniature town in order to enhance its realism. One of these later additions was the notorious bell that hung in the center of the town. It was originally a small school bell. The Ritters had purchased the bell from a local school. They felt that the bell would fit perfectly in their little town. It looked like it could be a normal-sized bell that was simply shrunk to the dimensions of their little town.

The Ritters themselves lived very close to the Handlebar Ranch. Their house sat on a hill just on the other side of Hughes Road from the Handlebar Ranch. Day and night, the Ritters could look down the hill from their windows and see the hayrides and festivities going on down in the town. A deck protruded through the forest's edge for a perfect view.

Throughout most of the 1970s, the Ritters were happy, and Handlebar Ranch was a successful business. All the children in the area knew about the ranch and would often beg their parents to let them go.

As the 1970s were coming to a close, things started to go badly for the attraction. Rumpke decided that it was going to create a large landfill for the city's garbage just up the road from the Handlebar Ranch. Many of the local people were very much against this, and they did whatever they could to stop it from happening. They knew that during the summer months, the stench from the mountain of garbage that would form would be unbearable. Locals knew that local property value would go way down, so they did everything in their power to stop Rumpke from moving into the area.

The Ritters contributed to this move against the landfill by telling the city that if Rumpke was allowed to build the landfill just up Hughes Road from the attraction, they would be forced to shut down the popular Handlebar Ranch. They stated that the children would be unable to have fun and participate in the fantasy town that they had created with the overwhelming smell of garbage hanging over their heads.

While the Ritters' plea to the town to stop the creation of the landfill helped to bring many more people against Rumpke, the move ultimately failed and the landfill was built anyway.

The Ritters attempted to keep Handlebar Ranch going over the next couple of years, but it had become an uphill battle. Attendance had recently gone down, and many operational costs had risen to unacceptable levels. The Ritters had to watch their once-successful hayride slowly fail. From their porch overlooking the tiny fantasy town, they could see that it was turning into just a shell of what it had once been.

In August 1978, the Ritters had finally had enough. They decided that it was time to shut down the hayrides and go out of business. The locals pleaded with them to keep the rides open, but Percy Ritter stated that insurance costs had risen to a point where they were too high. He said he hoped the closing would be only temporary, but the Handlebar Ranch would never open again.

As the years passed and the hayride remained dormant, the townspeople began to forget about the old hayrides on Hughes Road. The Ritters continued to live in the house overlooking the ranch, but it became more of a depressing sight to them than the joyous sight it used to be.

As more and more years passed, people who had never known the Handlebar Ranch as a hayride began to wonder what this interesting little town actually was. Active imaginations turned the pioneer village built as a children's attraction into a town built by retired circus little people. The town seemed so perfectly set up that people assumed that it was an actual town built by shorter people. The colors on the walls were so bright and vibrant that people assumed that they were circus colors to remind its inhabitants of their former jobs.

The legends would soon get out of control, and local vandals and teenagers would often enter the town at night and knock on the doors and ring the bell. This would always wake the Ritters, who lived just up the hill in an overlooking house. Sometimes the frustrated Ritters would yell down at the trespassers to get out of the Handlebar Ranch. If the trespassers still would not leave, the Ritters would sometimes throw stones or sticks down at them to get them to leave.

Teenagers who went to the town thinking that it was a town filled with circus little people could easily mistake the angry Ritters for midgets in the town. If the teenagers were unaware of the house hidden on the forested hill, the distant voices could sound higher pitched like they would imagine little people's voices would sound. And as soon as they began to get pelted by rocks and sticks, they would have run away without looking back at whom was actually throwing the projectiles at them.

Unfortunately, it seemed like the efforts of the Ritters to save their little town from trespassers only enhanced the legends. The more they tried to scare the trespassers away, the more the trespassers would come back to experience the unique legends about the small town.

The Handlebar Ranch, or Tiny Town as it became known to the locals who did not know its true history, sat dormant and decaying until 2008. Finally, the stark contrast between what the Handlebar Ranch used to be and what it had become became too much for the Ritters to bear. They built the oddity out of a love of children. They created it as a place of fun and joy. Over the years it became a place of crime and delinquency. People no longer regarded it as a place of fun but as a place of mystery and decay. By 2008, there was no longer any place within those brightly painted wooden walls for memories. The fun and joy that used to inhabit this place were gone—completely forgotten.

Early in 2008, the Handlebar Ranch was destroyed. The sign, the buildings, the small school bell, and Tiny Town were no more. The house on the hill overlooking the ruins of the town is gone as well. Just a concrete foundation remains, still standing sentinel, looking down the hill at the site it spent so many years protecting.

Short stone walls and shards of wood are all that remain of the town. An old wooden bridge with a wagon wheel gate still sits rusted and open on one end. The rest is gone, looking almost like an archeological site, just the foundations of what appears to have been a small town.

Perhaps the ruins will remain on the site and no further development will occur there. Perhaps everyone will again forget about this place and all the legends will fade away with the juggernaut of time. Perhaps one day in the far future an archaeologist will happen upon the site and will marvel at how small all the buildings were in this small town. Perhaps he will then come up with his own idea of who would inhabit such a small town.

Perhaps a ghost of this place will clue him in. He will hear the distant laughter of children, the last memory of joy long locked within a shard of brightly painted wood.

Lick Road: Amy's Ghost

As one approaches State Route 27 on West Kemper Road in the pitch of midnight, a faded yellow warning sign speaks more than it originally intended. Its reflective face is faded, dripped clean after many years of rain. The reflection of one's headlights seems to course down the sign's face like viscous blood. While the original purpose of the sign was to warn of an approaching right turn, a black arrow shaped like a quarter circle, its true effect on one who approaches it at night is the haphazard letters scrawled in ghostly reflective paint that simply say a name. Amy.

The Ritters would watch teenagers trespassing into the Handlebar Ranch from their house, pictured here. As the teenagers would ring the bell and wake them during the night, the Ritters would yell down and toss small rocks at the children. Perhaps the distant yells of the Ritters and the rocks being tossed at them from an unseen source convinced the locals that someone truly lived in this small town. In 2008, both the town and the home of the Ritters were torn down. As one drives down Hughes Road today there is only an empty field where the Handlebar Ranch once sat and only a concrete foundation where this house once stood. Only the locals know what once stood here.

Locals claim that is the name of the ghost who haunts this place. Amy—three simple letters have inspired countless ghost enthusiasts to park at the end of that road at night in hopes of experiencing one of the chilling tales that inhabit those woods.

Lick Road sits in Colerain Township off Kemper Road in the shadow of Mount Rumpke. It is in the northern reaches of the township—near the border of Butler County. At this point of Kemper Road, the asphalt stretches through rather desolate countryside. Here between the accident-prone intersection with Pippin Road and a deadly stretch of State Route 27, Kemper runs virtually unlit through the woods. Only the occasional farmhouse and a bar send artificial light out onto the road. The moon is constantly absent, perhaps swallowed by the surrounding trees.

From Kemper Road, Lick Road stretches deeper into the forest. It cuts northward, once a section of Bank Lick Road. Bank Lick Road was one of the major avenues of travel from Hamilton County into Butler County, but it fell out of favor when State Route 27 was built close by. Now Lick Road extends only about a mile into the woods before stopping at a rusted park gate.

Despite the fact that a bridge sits just beyond the gate spanning the creek and leading northward to Ross Township, the road is closed at that point. The old metal and asphalt bridge was closed down years ago. It was deemed unsafe by the township. It is now just a decrepit piece of the Richardson Nature Preserve.

This road, these woods, and this bridge are where Amy lives—or perhaps lives is the wrong word. These eerie surroundings are where the spirit of Amy echoes through the years.

Unfortunately, these echoes have the feel of unhappiness and terror.

The legends are never entirely clear about who exactly Amy was in life. One account tells of two lovers who frequented this secluded part of the township. For some reason or another, the two of them got into a terrible fight. In the heat of the quarrel, he struck her and she fell back. The exact cause of her death in this scenario is unclear. Some say she hit her head on a jagged piece of metal when she fell back. Some say that she was impaled by a tree limb that was protruding from the ground where she fell. But in this account, she was somehow killed by her lover during a heated argument on Lick Road. The story says that in a panic he left, and her body was later discovered on the abandoned bridge beyond the gate.

Other accounts say that Amy was not killed by her lover, but was a young hitchhiker who was picked up and murdered along Kemper Road by strangers.

The only concurrent point in the accounts seems to be that her body somehow ended up at that secluded bridge beyond the gate. The stories all agree that she died young and unexpectedly and that she was later discovered on that abandoned bridge in the woods.

Most places as desolate and lonely as this will often generate ghosts, and, according to legend, sometime after this young girl's murder, strange occurrences began happening down near the end of this gated-off road.

The most popular account of her haunting occurs near the gate at the end of Lick Road. Many different accounts report the same phenomena occurring. What happens is that someone drives their car and parks it at the end of the road. After several minutes, the windows will fog up. Slowly, as if someone outside the car is writing on the window, the word "Help" will appear in the condensation. Upon further investigation, there is no one outside the car. On top of that, the condensation is on the inside of the windows so whoever wrote the message had to have written it from the inside.

Does Amy need help or is this a message that repeats through the years like a broken record of her final moments of terror? Or is this just an urban legend that has fascinated the locals for years?

Other accounts of hauntings are equally eerie.

Once a group of amateur ghost hunters drove down to the end of Lick Road and parked their car. One girl in the group carried a video camera with her so that she could record anything that

Driving down Kemper Road seems perfectly normal while the sun is out, but if one passes through at night something very strange catches the eye. This small sign that warns motorists of the curve ahead also warns of the ghost that resides at the end of Lick Road. When a passing car's headlights shine on the sign, the word Amy appears. The ink appears to be dripping down the sign, and the letters run together. According to the legend, Amy was a hitchhiker who was picked up by several strangers, driven to the bridge at the end of Lick Road, and murdered there. Although historically there does not seem to be any evidence of a girl named Amy who died near Lick Road, there was a hitchhiker named Linda Dyer who was stabbed and strangled to death on a small secluded bridge nearby.

they experienced. After having parked for a few minutes, everyone in the car suddenly became very uncomfortable, like there was some evil presence all around them. Suddenly, they looked out and they all saw a bright glowing orb hovering near the car. The orb slowly circled the car several times as the group watched in wonder. Eventually the orb vanished without a trace and the feeling of discomfort left them.

They all began talking about what the glowing orb could have been. They wondered if it had been someone walking around with a flashlight or perhaps it was some kind of reflection of the ambient light. They decided to check the video camera so that they could try to get a better look at what it was. To their surprise, the video camera did not catch the orb at all. It recorded only the darkness despite having been pointed at the orb the entire time.

A man tells another story of a Lick Road haunting. He had driven to the dead end and had been sitting there for a half hour. He had heard the stories of Amy and was waiting for any sign of the supposed ghost. As he and his friends let the windows fog up, he heard faint footsteps in the gravel outside the car. Figuring one of the locals from the house down the road had approached his car, he stepped out to find the gravel around his car vacant. There was no one there. He and his friends investigated the immediate area but found nothing. Confused, he and his friends headed back to the car. Just before he opened his door to get in, a clear female voice echoed through the night, "I've had enough." The man looked around to see that his friends had heard it too. There was no one else around and no females in the group.

Another group of friends reported that while sitting at the end of the road with their windows down, they heard a strange echo. Then, shortly after, when they tried to roll up their automatic windows, the windows did not work.

Other strange stories run rampant in the area. Often, dark figures are seen disappearing into the woods. Are they just a trick of the light, or are they apparitions, reminders of the horrible thing that supposedly happened on this bridge? Ghostly footsteps on the path leading to the bridge and on the bridge itself have also been frequently reported. Are these sounds echoes of the witness's own footsteps, audible tricks of the creek down below the path, or does Amy follow people down that forsaken path during the dark hours of the night?

Life seems to lurk in the woods. Whether the stories about these ghosts are true or not, the woods seem to be alive. The shadows of every tree, the final twinkle from a distant light, and the sounds of the flowing creek below all amplify the sense that one who walks this haunted gravel is not alone there.

Perhaps one is never alone when walking Lick Road at night.

So is Amy real or are all these stories simply myths that locals have fabricated? The answer is probably more complicated than a simple yes or no. There are aspects of the legend that do have basis in historical fact, while there are other facets that seem to have come about through a misinterpretation of events.

According to our research, there was never a girl named Amy who was killed on Lick Road. In fact, it seems as if there was never a young girl's body found on the bridge. While these facts seem to discredit the legends behind Amy's ghost, an incident occurred very near the site that is eerily similar to many of the stories behind the Lick haunting. It is the tragic story of Linda Dyer.

Linda Dyer was a 15-year-old girl from Cincinnati who joined her friends at a party in Monfort Heights on August 24, 1976. Earlier that night, Dyer had left her jacket at a local bar and wanted to find a way back there to recover it. She asked her friends, but they refused to leave the party to drive her out to the bar. Dyer and her friends got into a huge fight, yelling at one another until Dyer, frustrated, decided that she was going to hitchhike her way back to the bar to get her jacket.

She hitchhiked outside the party near North Bend Road until a car finally stopped to pick her up. Two men pulled up in an orange 1975 Volkswagen. Dyer asked them if they could drive her out to the bar where she had left her jacket. They agreed, and she jumped into their car. She was never seen alive again.

Later that night, a resident of Colerain would report that she heard something happen during the night. Just across Kemper Road from Lick Road there was an area that the local resident said was popular with teenagers. She reported that on that particular night she had heard a lot of voices coming from the area. She said that the only thing she could understand that they said was something about alcohol. Nothing else was clear enough to understand. The last thing she remembered was seeing a couple of cars drive away from the area.

It was not until 6:30 p.m. the following day that Dyer's body was found. The Colerain Township police received a telephone call from a crew that was working on a bridge at the corner of Crest and Bank Roads. While working, they had discovered a nude female body underneath the bridge. They described her as an 18–25 year old white girl. She was about five feet, four inches tall and had brown hair and brown eyes. When the police arrived, they discovered nothing on her person that could reveal her identity.

There was no blood in the area surrounding the body, which led investigators to believe that she had been killed elsewhere and her body was dumped here. The cause of death was a stab wound. Investigators estimated that she had been dead for about 24 hours due to the degree of decomposition.

The autopsy revealed that she had been stabbed and strangled to death at some point during the previous evening. Without any clues toward the victim's identity, the police contacted the local papers and encouraged them to release a sketch of what the victim looked like. They hoped that in identifying the victim, they could discover her whereabouts the night before and perhaps find out with whom she was last seen.

A full two weeks passed before the coroner's office was able to identify the body. Through dental records, they were able to identify her as Linda Dyer. Since nearly two weeks had passed since her disappearance, it was nearly impossible for police to get detailed information on the two men who had likely killed her. All that the witnesses could remember was that two men in an orange Volkswagen had driven her away from the party. Her jacket had never been picked up from the bar where she had left it.

With no leads, the police gave up on finding the murderers. The case is still listed as unsolved and is filed away in a cold case file somewhere in the city.

So perhaps the famous ghost of Amy who haunts the woods at the end of Lick Road is actually the ghost of Linda Dyer. One of the legends about the origin of Amy was that she was a young girl who was hitchhiking and was killed by the men who picked her up. This is probably exactly what happened to Dyer. The bridge at which Dyer's body was discovered was only about a mile from the bridge that Amy supposedly haunts. On top of this, Dyer was probably killed somewhere nearby and then dumped at the site where they found her.

It is not impossible that the murderers parked the car down at the secluded end of Lick Road while they raped and murdered Dyer and then drove a short distance to dump the body.

Ghosts are usually created from traumatic experiences, and again, Linda Dyer fits this profile. She was kidnapped by strangers, driven to a secluded area that she probably was not familiar with, raped, strangled, and stabbed. It is hard to imagine much that could have been more traumatic than this ordeal that Linda Dyer had to suffer. Perhaps she is haunting the area until her killers are brought to justice. Despite all the time that has passed, her murder still remains unsolved. There are many reasons that Linda Dyer's ghost could haunt the area.

The origin of the name Amy probably came from the street sign near Lick where her name is painted. It is an eerie sight when driving by the sign at night. But what came first, the ghost stories or the sign? It is difficult to pinpoint a time when the stories of the ghost of Amy began, but it is certainly possible that a vandal had scrawled the name on the sign as a tribute to a

In 1978, Lick Road was a road named Bank Lick Road, which expanded all the way into Butler County. However, less than 500 feet beyond where the road dead ends there is a small bridge that was deemed unsafe for vehicular travel. This bridge has since been overcome by the nearby forest. Spanning a small creek, this bridge and the nearby land is the property of Richardson Nature Preserve. The ghost of Amy is said to reside here. Legends say that Amy was murdered on this bridge. People will report hearing a girl's voice and footsteps as they stand here. Trespassing in this area is strictly forbidden, and due to the number of locals who want to see Amy, these laws are well enforced.

girlfriend, and witnesses to the phenomena at the end of Lick Road assumed that it was the name of the ghost.

Whatever the case, it does seem that this secluded place at the end of this rural road is haunted. There are too many cases where someone experiences something otherworldly. Whose spirit actually inhabits this dark place is still up for debate. While it is certainly possible that a girl named Amy was killed there at some point in history, it seems more likely that the ghost is actually that of Linda Dyer.

If history is passed orally from person to person, it can sometimes become distorted or the details blurred. Many of the historical details of Linda Dyer's tragic death have a strong similarity to that of the fictional Amy. It seems that over time only the name has changed, perhaps influenced by the surreal sign on Kemper Road.

Perhaps the ghost at the end of Lick Road will not rest until her killers are brought to justice. Or perhaps she will not rest until the world knows who she really is.

In 1975, Linda Dyer was heading home from a party in Montfort Heights when she realized she had left her jacket at a bar. Her friends refused to drive her to the bar so she decided she would hitchhike her way back. Two men in a Volkswagen picked her up and drove away. That was the last time her friends and family ever saw her alive. Nearly 24 hours later, some local surveyors reported a dead body lying in this small ditch at the intersection of Bank and Crest Roads under this small overpass. An autopsy revealed her death was caused by strangulation and stabbing. Police sketches were plastered all over the newspapers in hopes of determining who she was. It took more than two weeks before she was finally identified as Linda Dyer. Her killers were never brought to justice; the case is open to this day.

Two

ALONG THE GREAT MIAMI RIVER

Some faiths describe hell as a place that is filled with fire and suffering. Other faiths describe it as a place that is constantly dark and eerie, gloomy and cold. There are some places on earth where one can feel the evil resonate from every corner. These places are not fiery, but sometimes fires burn there. These places are not dark—at least not all the time.

Buffalo Ridge: Satan's Minions

High above where Dent, Miamitown, and Cleves all intersect, there is a hill that looks down on them all. The lights of the highway, the towns, and civilization all twinkle quite beautifully below. At the ridge's base, the Great Miami River meanders southward toward the Ohio River.

Thick forests still populate the crest of the ridge. The road that bears the same name, Buffalo Ridge Road, was recently repaved and widened. What once was a road without any lines to distinguish lanes is now a well-maintained residential street that gives those families that live along it better access to both Wesselman and East Miami River Roads, both near a major interstate.

Despite this attempt at urbanization, the road is still black at night. The thick foliage reaches like an awning over the road, cutting down the dim light from the moon and stars. The darkness of the road is overwhelming, and artificial lights from a car's headlights hardly remedy this.

The Mitchell Memorial Forest sits at the center of the road. Signs line the road as one nears its middle, warning that one is riding along the edge of a county park. The signs warn of excessive fines for littering along the road, and some say that trespassing is forbidden along certain trails that branch off from the main stretch. The forest is thick along the asphalt. Only the first line of trees is visible; anything behind them is lost in the dark.

Perhaps the trees are sentinels, guarding the forest's secrets from any passersby. They stand there night after night, week after week, season after season, year after year, motionless—essentially unchanging.

Some of the houses along the road appear abandoned. The front facade of some of these houses seems to have crumbled into disrepair, and all sorts of miscellaneous garbage litters the front yards. Broken-down cars, on cinder blocks, sit in the yard alone. One such house near Wesselman Road crumbles, abandoned, near the roadside. This house is reputed to be haunted. Many times when people drive by the house at night, they see that the lights are on. Sometimes they see a silhouette of an old woman in the window. Electricity had been shut off to the house long ago. There is no earthly explanation for the lights and the old woman.

Some of the houses are occupied. They sit back from the road in treeless fields, their lights on at night to guard against the evil that haunts the ridge.

Several legends circulate wildly about the dark history of Buffalo Ridge. The first such legend is that the ridge was the meeting place for a clan of Satan worshipers who used to hold

Buffalo Ridge is a creepy road from the moment one turns onto it. After the sun has set, the trees shade out all possible light and cast unusual shadows along the road. Despite this eerie sensation, many families call this road home. Near the bottom of the ridge by Wesselman Road, several small houses silently rest. These houses have been abandoned for many years. Many of them display broken windows and collapsing roofs. The house depicted here is reputed to be haunted. Electricity has not gone to this house since the last family left it; however, passing motorists frequently report seeing lights on in the house. Sometimes, when the lights turn on, people will also see a black figure standing in the window. It is an elderly woman; some say a witch.

As one approaches the crest of the ridge, a small wooden post with a chain attached to it tells people that trespassing beyond that point is strictly forbidden. The forest is owned by Hamilton County Parks and is a part of Mitchell Memorial Forest County Park. Farther into the woods, the ruins depicted here lay hidden by the foliage. Legend says a crematorium burned to the ground many years ago at this site; however, these ruins are actually the foundation of an unfinished planetarium. The Cincinnati Astronomical Society planned to build this planetarium just off Buffalo Ridge but eventually gave up on the project. The stones were simply abandoned in the forest.

ceremonies during the night. In the woods just off Buffalo Ridge Road, these Satanists used to hold elaborate ceremonies, which included huge bonfires and loud chanting. Some say that these Satan worshipers even performed human sacrifices during these ceremonies.

There is no concrete historical evidence that these ceremonies ever took place, although there are those who have ventured off into the forest and found rabbits and other small forest creatures that appear to have been ceremonially drained of blood.

Some historic artifacts in the area suggest that the ceremonies were a myth created by overactive imaginations. In the woods are all that remain of one of the great architectural wonders to ever stand in the city of Cincinnati. They are the marble and granite ruins of the chamber of commerce building, which stood on Fourth and Vine Streets in the early 1900s.

From 1889 until 1911, the chamber of commerce building stood higher than most buildings that surrounded it. It was made from granite and marble, with several towers that stood at its corners. Atop each of the towers was a large cross. The roof of the building peaked at a point higher than most of the buildings in the city. The roof could be seen from miles around. It made this building one of the defining landmarks of the city's downtown.

That was until 1911 when tragedy struck. Inexplicably, a fire broke out in the building and quickly spread. By the time firefighters could reach the scene, the fire was out of control. No matter what they did, the firefighters could not control the blaze. They had to wait until the fire had almost completely destroyed the inside of the building before they were able to put it out. The building was deemed unsalvageable and had to be destroyed.

A lot of the most beautiful parts of the building were untouched though. Since the outside facade was made of marble and granite, the outside of the building did not burn. There were carvings and sculptures that were still in the same condition as they were in before the fire.

The Cincinnati Astronomical Society took possession of this marble and granite and moved it out to the forest on Buffalo Ridge where they hoped to build an observatory with these remains. In 1911, Buffalo Ridge would have made a perfect place for an observatory since it was on a dark hill away from the city lights. The observatory never came to fruition, though, so the astronomical society attempted to build a planetarium with the stones. When they realized they did not have the interest or the resources to create a successful planetarium, the astronomical society ended up donating the stones to the Hamilton County Park District.

All throughout the county parks, one can still find pieces of the chamber of commerce building. In Eden Park there is a bridge known as the Melan Arch Bridge, which was constructed in 1894. Since the remains of the commerce building were donated to the parks, four stone eagle sculptures now decorate the ends of the bridge. These eagles were once a part of the chamber of commerce building.

Many other shelters and such throughout the park district are constructed using marble and granite left over from the fire.

The stones that were never used still sit in the woods on Buffalo Ridge. A trail leads into the woods off Buffalo Ridge, which is officially part of Mitchell Memorial Forest County Park. A Keep Out sign warns people not to walk down the path. Down that path lies what remains of the chamber of commerce building.

These remains do not look like a building any longer at all. Every once in a while there is a stone slab lying haphazardly in the mud. One of these slabs appears as if it has been struck repeatedly with some heavy blunt object like a hammer or an axe, and it appears to have blood-colored stains in the center.

Anyone who might venture into this part of the woods and find these strange marble slabs without knowing their history might assume that they were altars used in some strange ceremony. It is possible that the rumors of satanic rituals occurring in this forest were an urban legend whose origin was these slabs of marble. But this is not necessarily the case.

Strange things still do occur deep in the forest at night. Sometimes people will hear rhythmic chanting coming from deep in the woods. People will often hear screams coming from the darkness of the forest as well. Sometimes it will appear as if a large fire is burning somewhere deep in the woods, but if one tries to approach the fire, it will mysteriously vanish. Perhaps these are all paranormal remnants of actual satanic rituals that once occurred in this dark place.

Another famous legend of Buffalo Ridge is that of a haunted crematorium that sits in the forest. Unfortunately, this is another legend that is a twisting of actual history. There was never a crematorium on the ridge, but if one was to hike back into the forest there is a structure there that now sits in ruins.

Again, this is part of the chamber of commerce building. When the Cincinnati Astronomical Society thought better of building its observatory, it actually made plans and began building a planetarium for the people of Cleves and Cincinnati to come and enjoy. Only the foundation was completed before the astronomical society scrapped the idea. The unfinished building somehow gained the reputation in the area of being a crematorium that burned down in the early part of the 20th century. The legends about its origin are untrue, but several ghostly happenings have occurred near the unfinished planetarium.

Once a group of boys was traveling out to the site at night to look for ghosts. They were using only flashlights to guide their way. Slowly they were able to make their way into the woods, and as they came within sight of the planetarium, they felt a change in the air, like something was not right. They entered the ruins. Almost immediately, they all saw a black shadowy figure approaching them from the forest. The group was immediately concerned. They knew that unsavory people would often use the area at night to drink and party. The group of boys was concerned that they had trespassed onto the turf of some dangerous people.

The black shadowy figure approached them quickly and aggressively before suddenly disappearing into thin air just 10 feet in front of them. Frightened, the group ran out of the forest and back to the car.

These are not the only ghosts that populate the ridge though. There are many other stories that are recounted just as often about the haunted ridge.

Perhaps the most popular ghost story of the ridge is the story of the white van. One time there was a couple that was driving down Buffalo Ridge Road from East Miami River Road toward Wesselman Road. When their car neared Zion Road near the top of the ridge, a white van suddenly pulled up behind the couple and started to tailgate them. The road is dark and quite curvy at night, so the couple became quite worried about their safety as the van's headlights shone brightly through their back window. They could not go any faster in order to lose the van since the road was so curvy, and they were terrified that if they went any slower, the van would hit them in the bumper.

They moved farther and farther down the road in a panic. They were unable to see anyone in the van behind them through its dark windows, and the van only seemed to loom closer and closer to them. But then suddenly, as they crested a hill, the van simply vanished. There were no houses or roads in the area. There was nowhere the van could have turned off. It simply disappeared without a trace.

These two people in the car were not the only witnesses to the white van on Buffalo Ridge. There are many different accounts where the car is tailgated by the white van, and then the van vanishes without warning.

Since the beginning of the road, there have been many car accidents up on the ridge. Some of these car accidents have resulted in fatalities. There is another story that circulates about Buffalo Ridge and a group of teenagers who were killed in a gang initiation stunt. The story goes that the driver of the car was supposed to drive as quickly as he could from one end of Buffalo Ridge to the other. During the race, a slow-moving car happened to be just beyond one of the road's many blind corners. Unable to stop, the teenager driving the car could only swerve around the slow-moving vehicle. Unfortunately, the roads were too curvy, and the teenager lost control of the vehicle and slammed into a tree at high speed. Everyone in the car was killed.

It is impossible to tell whether or not the story is true. There have been fatal accidents on the ridge, but whether or not the accident on record is the accident in this story is difficult to determine. But again, whether or not it is true, there are ghost stories that involve this particular gang initiation story.

Sometimes when people are driving along Buffalo Ridge, a white car will suddenly turn the corner behind them. The white car will pass the surprised driver and lose control as they go around the next corner. The unsuspecting driver who was passed hears screams and a car wreck up ahead. As the driver moves farther up the road expecting to see a terrible car accident, he or she is surprised to find nothing there. There are no signs of any car accident, and there are no signs that any car had even been there.

Drivers are not the only witnesses to this particular haunt. People who live in some of the houses along the road will sometimes hear a car accident and screams during the night and not see an accident out on the road. The next morning when they look into it and check the news and local papers for a report of the accident, they find no record of it.

One of the creepiest haunts of Buffalo Ridge also involves an accident up on the ridge. Locals remember a terrible school bus accident that occurred on the ridge during the 1950s. Somehow or another the school bus lost control during one of the road's many curves and hills and ended up crashing. Locals remember the bus accident being a big deal in the community because a couple of the children on the bus were killed.

Once a couple parked their car on Buffalo Ridge Road near Zion Road. They had planned to sit up there and admire the stars, but soon after they had parked things began to get intimate between them. The windows fogged up as things progressed. Suddenly they heard footsteps outside their car in the darkness. Since the windows had fogged up, the guy in the car straightened himself up and then opened his door to see who was there. The road was quite remote, and he was curious who was out this late at this spot. They had not seen any headlights, so whoever was walking outside the car had to have walked there.

He opened the door and looked outside. There was only gravel out there. He grabbed a flashlight from the car and shone it into the adjacent woods but saw nothing. He was getting nervous by this point. The entire place had seemed to take on an ominous feeling that was not there when they had parked there. He tried to start the car, but it would not start.

The footsteps started again, and this time they seemed much closer to the vehicle. Both of them were quite scared by this point, so he did not open the door to go check what was out there. He tried to start the car again. As the car started up, little children's handprints began appearing in the condensation on the windows. The condensation was on the inside of the windows; the handprints could not have been coming from children outside. And even if there were children out there, what were they doing in this remote section of the road that late at night?

He finally got the car started and sped out of there as quickly as he could. Other people since have reported the children's handprints in the condensation on their windows.

Another ghost story involves a demon dog that has been seen near the intersection of Buffalo Ridge and Zion Road. Once a car was approaching the intersection but had to stop short because a tan-colored dog was slowly crossing the street in front of them. As they waited for the dog to cross out of their way, it suddenly stopped and looked over at the car. Its eyes were glowing a fiery red color. The dog moved to the edge of the road and started eating the grass at the edge of the forest. Terrified, the car drove away.

Another popular story that comes from the ridge involves the Mitchell Memorial Forest County Park. The park itself is a 1,335-acre park that sits atop Buffalo Ridge. The entrance to the park is actually on Zion Road, but much of the forest along Buffalo Ridge Road is part of the park. The

A man named William Morris Mitchell owned the land where Mitchell Memorial Forest is today. When Mitchell donated this land to the Hamilton County Parks, he made them promise that all the land he donated to them would remain a part of that park and would never be sold to the public. The Hamilton County Park District agreed to this, and Mitchell Memorial Forest became a county park. After some time passed, William Morris Mitchell passed away and a nearby resident wanted to purchase a pond that sat adjacent to his property but was officially part of the park. He offered the county a great deal of money for the pond, and the Hamilton County Parks agreed to this purchase despite Mitchell's request. Since that point, the once calm and peaceful pond has become black and turbulent. Perhaps this is the spirit of William Morris Mitchell, angry that his conditions for the donation were not met.

marble and granite left over from the chamber of commerce building is currently sitting abandoned within the boundaries of the park.

The park was created through the generosity of a man named William Morris Mitchell. Mitchell purchased the land and helped to finance its creation into a park. He wanted to donate all this to the county as a tribute to his parents, who had died.

From here it is unclear what is local legend and what is fact, but the stories say that as a stipulation of the donation, Mitchell insisted that none of the land be sold off to the private sector. He insisted that all the land remain a government park. Almost as soon as Mitchell died, though, the county sold a small section on the outskirts of the park to a private homeowner. The section that was sold held a small pond, and the homeowner was willing to pay a large price to incorporate the pond into his property.

At the time of the sale, the pond was a beautiful and clear pond. It was tranquil and shimmering all throughout the year, so the homeowner considered it a very wise purchase that would greatly increase the value of his home.

After the sale, the pond completely changed. Many of the locals claim that this change was due to the ghost of William Morris Mitchell. Since Mitchell was very clear about his wish that none of the park be sold off to the public, they say that his spirit is angry about this sale and it constantly haunts the pond.

The pond can be easily seen from Buffalo Ridge Road. It is in a clearing and is the only body of water that can be seen from the road itself. Today it is anything but tranquil and clear. Today the water is very dark. It is so dark that it looks almost black. It is also very turbulent. It appears as if a multitude of small vortices are spinning out of control within the pond. Nothing seems to have happened to the pond to make it this way. Nothing flows into the pond to account for the turbulence. The locals know what happened though. They know that Mitchell will not be happy until the pond is returned to the park. Only then will the ghost of Mitchell rest. Only then will the darkness that has enveloped the pond allow it to return to its original clear, tranquil self.

A final legend actually takes place on East Miami River Road, right where it meets Buffalo Ridge Road. The legend says that sometimes people will see a headless woman, dressed in a wedding dress, looking for her missing head. According to the stories, the ghost will only appear on the anniversary of her death to continue this search for her missing head.

Remarkably, this strange story holds some striking similarities to a piece of recent history in the area. A woman lived in a trailer on East Miami River Road with her boyfriend and her two sons. After having been with him for a very long time and having two children with him, her boyfriend finally proposed to her. It appeared as if she was finally going to get married.

A few days later, while they were still in the stages of making wedding plans, a terrible accident occurred on I-275 on an overpass that crossed East Miami River Road. A semitruck hit the woman's car as she crossed the overpass, and her car slammed into the guardrail. Witnesses pulled over their cars to rush to her to offer any assistance that they could. When the witnesses approached the car, they realized to their horror that the woman had been decapitated. Perhaps the woman from this accident is the headless woman in the wedding dress that walks East Miami River Road on the anniversary of her death.

Just a few years later, further tragedy would destroy the remainder of this woman's family. A mysterious fire broke out in the family's trailer one day. The boyfriend was barely able to escape with his life, but both of the children were killed in the blaze.

Buffalo Ridge feels evil. The trees swallow all light. Darkness looks on menacingly from the forest. It is impossible to tell what lies beyond that first row of trees as one is driving by. It is impossible to tell whether the scream one heard was real or a trick of the acoustics.

The smoke from the dark ceremonies, the crematorium, and that fiery bus accident still might choke one who unsuspectingly steps on these sacred grounds.

Miamitown: Sacred Hunting Ground

There is a legend that is alive in Miamitown. Actually, it is probably more of a ghost story, but so many of the historic details have been lost that it works more like a legend. The only proof of the story lies in oral tradition, and the exact location of the story has been lost to history. It is a story worth telling though. It almost defines how the living element and the spiritual element of this small town interact.

In the 1800s, there was a house in Miamitown that was haunted. It was not just haunted; it was very violently haunted. When the sun went down, the family who lived in this house was constantly under assault by the spirit's aggressive nature.

Once, while the family was eating dinner, the dishes lifted off the table by themselves and flew into the wall, sending shards of porcelain across the room. As the family watched in horror, the cabinets opened by themselves, and the dishes inside the cabinets began hurling themselves across the room. The family retreated to the next room as the remainder of the dishes shattered against the walls.

Another attack happened while the mother was in the attic of the house straightening up. The attic of this house was a nice finished attic, almost like another floor of the home with nice hardwood floors and a fireplace. As the mother was cleaning the attic, something grabbed her by the hair and dragged her across the floor and down the stairs.

Whenever the children would attempt to enter the attic of this home, unseen hands would violently grab them by the arms, leaving hand-shaped bruises where the unseen spirit had grabbed them.

It quickly got to the point where the family involved in the haunting did not know what to do. The ghostly activity was getting more violent. Everyone in the family would get scratches from unseen sources, objects would inexplicably hurl themselves across the room at the parents and children, and all other manner of terrifying events would keep the family awake all night long.

The family could not just move, though. To move in that day and age would have been a tremendous undertaking. In those days, when people moved out to a pioneer town like Miamitown, they moved there and built their own houses with what little resources they had. People could not just sell their houses and move somewhere else because there was nowhere else to move. They could not just build another house because they did not have the money or the resources to leave the one they had.

The town decided that it would help this poor family. People from around the area felt that the only way to stop these hauntings would be to somehow communicate with the ghosts, so some people from the town came to the house on Halloween night to hold a séance, in hopes of contacting whatever malevolent entities might be terrorizing the family. The townspeople sat around a table in the attic, the room where many felt the haunting was centered, and began their séance.

For hours they sat there and cried out, in a vain attempt to contact the ghosts. As the candlelight began to flicker and the townspeople were about to give up hope, an apparition appeared to all involved. The apparition was that of a young Native American woman. The townspeople asked her why she was terrorizing this household. They asked her why she was trying so hard to hurt this poor family. They asked her what that family had ever done to her. They asked her why she was so angry.

The spirit of the Native American woman answered that she was only looking for her baby.

The townspeople remembered a story that they had heard from many years back. Rumor was that a pioneer man and a Native American woman had had an affair. They had fallen in love and had carried on the affair in secret for many months. Eventually, though, the Native American woman became pregnant. Nine months later a child was born, and everything changed for the couple. In their time, it was unheard of that a pioneer and a Native American would have a child together. In order to save his own reputation and in a vain attempt to keep his affair with the woman secret, the pioneer stole the baby from its mother, carried it out into the woods, and smothered it to death so that it could not scream. He buried it in a shallow unmarked grave in the forest. Upon learning what had happened, the woman, crippled with grief, roamed the forest for days looking for her child. When she came to the realization that her child was dead and that she would never find it, she hung herself from a tree.

The townspeople assumed that this apparition at the séance was the Native American mother from that story. They told her that what she had to do was to move on to the next life. Once she moved on, she would find her child there. The woman agreed to do this. The townspeople stopped her from leaving right then, though. They told her that one year from that night, they would hold another séance. They wanted her to return during that séance and let them know whether she had found her baby.

At that moment, the remaining candles burned out and the attic went dark for a second. By the time anyone was able to light a lantern, the apparition had vanished.

The next morning the family returned to the house to see if the séance had succeeded in its goal of ridding the house of the ghost. To their excitement, the hauntings had completely stopped. The family was able to be at peace when they were in their home. They were grateful to the townspeople for getting rid of their violent ghost, but like the rest of the town, they had heard what had happened during the séance and were anxiously awaiting the next Halloween. They wanted to know as much as anyone whether or not the spirit had found her baby.

Finally, the night of the séance arrived. The same group of townspeople sat around the same table in the attic, and began to ask the spirit to show itself again. Again, hours passed without incident. The candles on the table had melted so low that they had started to flicker. Just as the dim light from the candles was about to extinguish itself, everyone in the room saw the apparition of the Native American woman.

In her arms she held an infant child.

Then it went dark.

While the exact location of this story has been lost to history, there is an antique shop on Route 128 where this story may have happened. A past owner of this antique shop had recently purchased it and was working hard to get everything ready for the opening day. As she was setting up she was perplexed that she could find no way to get into the attic of the building. From outside, she could clearly see that there was an attic to the building, but inside there were no stairs or crawl spaces or any way to get up into the attic.

Eventually she gave up on finding the attic and continued to arrange the antiques for opening day. As she was setting things up on the second floor, she noticed what looked like the outline of stairs on the wall. It was as if stairs had once been there and dust had gathered in the corner. The stairs had been removed, though, and would only have led into a wall.

The storeowner called her son and asked him to come to the shop and bust out the wall to see if there was an entry to the attic behind the wall. When he broke through the wall, the remainder of the stairs was still intact, and they led upward to the attic. When they went up into the attic they were amazed. It was like another floor to the building. There were hardwood floors and a nice fireplace.

Perhaps this is the same attic as was recounted in the story of the Native American mother. But if so, if the hauntings did actually stop after the séance, why would anyone board up an attic as nice as this?

While the Native American mother story is more of a myth that has been handed down in the small town from generation to generation, there are many ghosts in Miamitown that are still active and frighten passersby to this day. In fact, as early as the late 1700s, the land was considered haunted by settlers moving through the area. Rumor was that if one camped in the area after dark, one would not wake up the next morning.

This rumor had some basis in historic truth. The land on which Miamitown now sits was considered a sacred hunting ground to the Shawnee Indians in the 1700s. The Shawnee themselves would not camp in the area after dark because they believed that it was disrespectful to the animal spirits that haunted the area. The Shawnee found it disrespectful when the settlers from the east would camp in their sacred land, so oftentimes, after dark, they would sneak into the settlers' camps and kill the pioneers in their sleep. Many times pioneers foolish enough to camp in Miamitown in the 1700s would not wake up the next morning.

Eventually though, the Shawnee were forced out and the Europeans were able to settle the area. The first settler was a man named Arthur Henry, a nephew of the Revolutionary War hero Patrick Henry. Eventually the town grew around the intersection of Route 128 and Route 52, both major paths of transport in the 1800s. Churches, houses, general stores, and a cemetery eventually came to life in this little town that settlers had once feared to enter.

The cemetery is near the south side of the town. The Miamitown Municipal Cemetery has a rather dark history. In the 1950s, the Miamitown cemetery was on the eastern side of Route 128. Since the 1800s, it had sat in this location, just off the road, cozily tucked at the bottom of a small incline. This all changed when the township decided to build an elementary school. Residents decided that the best place to build the school would be the land where the cemetery was. They figured that it would be a simpler effort to move the cemetery across the street to the churchyard than to demolish and move any of the other buildings that were already lining 128.

It seemed as if it would be a straightforward undertaking. They would simply exhume the bodies that were buried underneath the tombstones, move the bodies across the street, and rebury them with the proper headstone. They figured that the dead would not be disturbed since everything would be replaced exactly as they had found it, only across the street. So this is exactly what they did; they meticulously exhumed each body with its proper headstone and moved them across the street to be reburied in the same manner.

It was not until construction began on the elementary school's parking lot that the true horror of these mistakes came to light. Apparently, throughout the existence of the cemetery, there had been people buried there without proper headstones. Oftentimes when people could not afford granite headstones with names and dates carved into them, the families would simply mark the body with a stone or a wooden marker. Stones get misplaced, and wooden markers deteriorate. It was also possible that some of the original stone headstones had simply broken and been removed throughout the cemetery's history.

As the workers began digging up the ground for the elementary school, they began digging up bodies. Stories go that it was not just one or two bodies that were discovered, there were piles and piles of bodies that were being dug up.

No one had any idea who these bodies were, but since they had already moved those bodies that still had markers across the street, the only thing that they could do with them was to move them. They carried the unidentified bodies in piles across the street and buried them without ceremony in unmarked graves.

The spirits of those whose bodies were moved in such a haphazard way still haunt both sides of 128. At night, people walking across the Miamitown Elementary School parking lot will feel a chill creep down their spine. People will feel as if they are being watched, but when they look around, there is no one there. Sometimes people will see shadowy figures move back and forth between the trees behind the lot or will hear phantom footsteps following them across the lot. Again, if these witnesses investigate further, they find that there is no one there.

A teacher at the Miamitown Elementary School recounts a story of her own. For some reason or another she had to go into the storage room in the basement of the school. She entered the storage room alone and began to gather the supplies that she needed. Suddenly, she got the sensation that she was being watched and chills crept painfully down her back. She quickly looked all around to see if there was anyone else in the room. Further into the closet, she saw a lady dressed all in gray. The lady in gray glared across the storage room at her. The teacher felt that the apparition wanted her out of the storage closet, so in a panic, the teacher fled the room.

The frightened teacher told some of her friends at the school about her encounter. The other teachers told her about their own encounters with the lady in gray. In all accounts, this lady is a menacing and ominous presence. Most of the teachers refuse to go into the storage closet in the basement by themselves for fear of encountering this lady in gray. Perhaps the spirit is the ghost of one of those who was buried at the site, restless because her grave had been moved across the street without a marker to lead her back to it.

The cemetery itself is also haunted. While those who were properly moved may still rest in peace, the spirits of those who were buried here without markers are restless to this day.

Townspeople will report being uncomfortable when walking through the grounds. They will hear footsteps and breathing behind them although there is no one there and will see shadows that look like figures moving from headstone to headstone. No reason for any of these phenomena is ever discovered.

The most commonly reported ghost in the cemetery is that of the girl in white. Often people will report seeing a little girl in a glowing white dress walking across the cemetery. Almost as soon as they see this girl, though, she vanishes. Perhaps this apparition is nothing more than the reflection of passing headlights on reflective headstones, or perhaps this girl in white is another apparition awakened by the move from across the street.

Ghosts seem to inhabit almost every dwelling, antique shop, and back road in Miamitown, but the town's most famous ghost forever crosses the bridge on the north end of the town.

The bridge that crosses the Great Miami River at Route 52 is the fourth bridge to cover that span of the river. The first bridge was an old covered bridge and a toll bridge that charged travelers as they would cross. Union general Ambrose Burnside's men destroyed this bridge during the Civil War. Morgan's Raiders was a group of cavalrymen from the Confederacy that crossed the Ohio River into Indiana. When Morgan's Raiders moved into Ohio, General Burnside ordered the Miamitown Bridge destroyed so that Gen. John Hunt Morgan and his men could not cross the Great Miami River there. General Morgan was forced to cross the river farther north, and as a result General Burnside was able to head him off east of Cincinnati and capture him.

In 1896, a second bridge was built over the same stretch of the Great Miami. This bridge was a large metal bridge that used large steel beams to hold the bridge up. This bridge stood for 92 years, and at least two fatal accidents occurred here.

The first accident on the bridge involved a wagon carrying hay. When farmers would travel distances with hay, a man was always supposed to sit atop the hay holding the stack stable to prevent any from falling off. As the wagon crossed the bridge, a car began coming from the other direction. The wagon was forced to swerve out of the way to avoid hitting the car, and the man on the back was thrown off the hay and into the river below. Unfortunately, his heavy work boots quickly filled with water and carried him to the bottom of the river, anchoring him to the riverbed. He drowned there right underneath the bridge as the gathering townspeople watched helplessly.

Another accident occurred during renovations of the bridge. The bridge was closed down, and the deck of the bridge was taken out in order for a more stable replacement deck to be installed. The only way to cross on the bridge was on the big steel I beams that had supported the grated decking.

Late one night, an intoxicated man stepped into his car near the bridge after a long night at the local bar. Not realizing that the bridge was closed down, he began to drive across the bridge on the metal I beams. Remarkably, he was able to make it halfway across the bridge before his front wheels fell off the beams. The truck fell forward slightly and became lodged between the beams, stranding him in the middle of the bridge. The drunk man in the truck wondered what had happened, so he opened his door and stepped out of his truck unaware of the fact that there was no bridge underneath his door. He fell out of his truck and into the river below where he drowned in the fierce undertow.

Eventually, this big steel bridge was considered an eyesore in the small town, so it was decided that a new bridge be built over the same span of the river. Since Route 52, Harrison Avenue, at this point carried a lot of traffic, officials decided to keep the flow of traffic running by building a temporary span over the river while they built the new permanent bridge. The temporary span was not meant to be a long-term fix since the permanent bridge was slated to be finished in less than a year. Pylons on the riverbed actually supported the temporary bridge. It held up without problem until late May 1989.

In May 1989, a series of storms had struck the Ohio River valley, and the rivers in the area had all swelled above flood stage. The Great Miami River itself was seven feet over flood stage, but more importantly, the river was carrying a lot of debris like downed tree branches. The branches were slamming up against the pylons. This debris coupled with the high river current concerned the engineer working on the new bridge.

On May 26, the engineer called the mayor of Whitewater Township and voiced his concern about the stability of the temporary span of the Miamitown Bridge. The mayor immediately telephoned local law enforcement and insisted that they shut down the bridge until the river went back down and any damage to the bridge could be assessed.

Within an hour of the engineer's call, the officer was able to get the barricade out to the bridge, but it was too late. A nearby dispatcher told them the bridge had already collapsed. Officially, three people perished in the bridge collapse. Two cars went into the Great Miami River. One car held a single driver who was found drowned in the car. The other car held a driver and a passenger. The driver was found drowned in the car, and the passenger was missing. It was days before the passenger was found; she had been washed almost eight miles down the river, to where Route 50 crossed the Great Miami.

Witnesses from that night and newspaper articles from the day after, report a third vehicle that went down with the bridge. People report that they saw a red truck fall into the river when it collapsed. No one ever reported a red truck missing, and a red truck was never found in the river. It was as if all the witnesses who saw the red truck had been mistaken.

It is likely that some of the ghostly tales that surround this bridge today are based on these tragedies. The most popular legend that accompanies this bridge is the story of a ghostly white figure that is oftentimes seen crossing the bridge from the east side to the west side. As the figure begins to cross the bridge, it is a very clear apparition, but as it nears the western shore, it gets less and less pronounced to the point where it disappears completely.

Old Native American myth says that spirits cannot cross water. Miamitown was a sacred hunting ground for the Shawnee Indians in the late 1700s. Perhaps the figure is the spirit of a Native American trying to cross the river but is unable because he cannot cross water.

Other legends tell of screams or voices around the bridge. Are these sounds just tricks of the acoustics, echoes of the water flowing below, or are they the spirits of those who have perished here at the Miamitown Bridge over these many years of its history? And what of the red truck? Was there really a red truck? Perhaps the driver, forever lost within the mud and silt of the Great Miami's riverbed, is that ghostly figure who still walks the bridge at night. Perhaps he is replaying his final moments, forever trying to get to wherever it was that he was going on that fateful May night in 1989.

This section of the Great Miami River has seen two bridges before this one. The first bridge to span this section was a covered bridge that required a toll to pass through. During the Civil War, Gen. Ambrose Burnside commanded his army to destroy the bridge to prevent Morgan's Raiders from crossing at that point and allowing General Burnside to head them off farther north. Several years later, in 1896, another bridge was constructed. The bridge was a large steel bridge that did not fit in with the surroundings. In 1988, town officials decided to tear this bridge down to build something a little less obtrusive. Harrison Avenue is a popular avenue of travel so they needed some way for motorists to cross the river while the new bridge was being built. This temporary bridge was constructed and lasted until a stormy day in May 1989. (Courtesy of the Whitewater Township Historical Society.)

On May 26, 1989, the Miamitown Bridge collapsed, killing at least three people. The month of May had seen many big storms and heavy winds. Debris was quickly rushing down the Great Miami River. As the debris slammed against the support pylons, the engineer working on the bridge decided that it needed to be shut down and the damage assessed. He called the township's mayor and told him to have the bridge shut down until the storms passed and the river calmed down. The mayor promptly contacted the local sheriff's office, and an officer was dispatched to shut it down. He grabbed his barricades and rushed off to the bridge. Just minutes before he arrived, he was notified that he was too late; the bridge had collapsed. Two cars went into the river, and three people died. This photograph depicts one of the ill-fated cars being pulled out of the river. (Courtesy of the Whitewater Township Historical Society.)

Congress Green Cemetery: The Ressurectionists

Despite its proximity to Cincinnati and its historical significance, many people from Cincinnati have never even heard of the village of North Bend. When the town was founded in 1789, its founder, John Cleves Symmes, had incredibly high hopes for the town. Symmes had purchased all the land in southern Ohio north of the Ohio River and between the Great Miami River and Little Miami River. He built his house in a beautiful spot where the Ohio River made a northerly turn and called his little town North Bend.

The late 1700s and early 1800s were booming times in southwestern Ohio. Symmes sold off a lot of his purchase to settlers, and many towns sprang up around North Bend. One of these towns that was founded using Symmes's land was called Losantiville. *Losantiville* was a word created from a mix of languages, meaning "land opposite the Licking River." Losantiville would be the city that destroyed Symmes's dreams of making North Bend the greatest city in southwestern Ohio. The town of Losantiville would eventually change its name to Cincinnati, and North Bend would slowly fade to Cincinnati's peripheries.

John Cleves Symmes accomplished a lot in his lifetime. He served the country as a judge in New Jersey during its infancy. He served on the Continental Congress. His son-in-law, William Henry Harrison, would become a great war hero and the president of the United States. Symmes was the founder of all the great towns and communities in southwestern Ohio. Historically, Symmes is remembered as a great and successful man. And despite how many towns around the area bear his name or how large the city that he founded named Cincinnati has become, North Bend will always be remembered as his town.

Before he died, one of the last things that he set up in his beloved North Bend was a cemetery. It was on a secluded little hill that overlooked the Ohio River. He called it the Pasture Graveyard, and when he died in 1814, he was one of the first people to be buried there. His is the oldest stone that still stands in the cemetery. It overlooks a spectacular view of the Ohio River and the Kentucky forests beyond.

In 1841, another grave site would be built just adjacent to the Pasture Graveyard. This grave site was of a man who was even more famous than Symmes. It was the grave of his son-in-law, William Henry Harrison. Harrison was a hero during Tecumseh's War in 1811, when he defeated Tecumseh's forces at the Battle of Tippecanoe. Harrison became a great American hero and eventually rose to the rank of president of the United States of America.

His term as president, though, would forever be remembered as one of the more tragic episodes of American history. During his inaugural address, Harrison contracted pneumonia and died only a couple of months later. William Henry Harrison would be the first president to die while in office.

Legends say that Harrison died because of a Native American curse that was placed on the American people because of their actions toward the native people. Since William Henry Harrison represented a huge defeat for the Native American cause, those who administered the curse warned that if William Henry Harrison ever became president of the United States, he would die in office and a president in every generation thereafter would also die while in office.

Those who believe in this Native American curse on the presidents of the United States point out the fact that from William Henry Harrison in 1841 to John Kennedy in 1963, every president that was elected on a 20-year mark died in office. Harrison died of pneumonia; Abraham Lincoln was shot in 1865; James Garfield was shot in 1881; William McKinley was shot in 1901; Warren G. Harding died of a heart attack in 1923; Franklin Roosevelt died in office in 1945; and John F. Kennedy was shot in 1963. People say that the curse was finally broken when Ronald Reagan was shot in 1981 but survived the assassination attempt.

When Harrison died in 1841, he was buried in a vault at the site that he had chosen himself. The tomb was a simple stone tomb with the name Harrison carved on the front of it. As the years went by and several more family members were buried in the vault, people became interested in the historical significance of the tomb. The State of Ohio gained ownership of the site in 1919 and built two pillars with sculptures of stone eagles on them that same year. In 1924, the tomb was redone in order to achieve the appearance that it has today. A 60-foot obelisk was added to the top of the tomb, making it one of the more imposing and impressive tombs in the country.

But despite the elegance, beauty, and historical significance of the William Henry Harrison tomb, it has a dark distinction of being the tomb of the first president to die in office and an imposing reminder of this curse that had plagued the American presidents for so many years. Perhaps Harrison's ghost still roams the area, frustrated at his inability to ever rule the country as president after all the hard work that he had to complete to achieve the office.

After the Civil War, Pasture Graveyard would have its name officially changed to Congress Green Cemetery. It is today one of the few locations in the world in which buffalo clover still grows wild. Buffalo clover used to be a huge presence in America, but as the buffalo population decreased due to increased hunting, the buffalo clover was unable to spread as much as it had. Today buffalo clover has nearly gone extinct, making this grouping of the plant at the cemetery important to the plant's survival. In this way, Congress Green Cemetery is also a botanically important place in southwestern Ohio.

By the end of the 19th century, this beautiful cemetery that held John Cleves Symmes and members of his family would take on a much darker identity. In 1878, something terrible would happen at Congress Green Cemetery that would define it historically until today.

This is due to a man named John Scott Harrison. But the story starts much earlier in history than him. It starts in England and America during the late 1700s. It was during this time that a group of thieves called the resurrectionists got their start.

In the late 1700s, there were many legitimate medical schools popping up all over the world. In order for these medical schools to operate properly, though, they needed real human bodies. The students needed to see the inside workings of the human body so that they could better understand how to fix it.

Unfortunately, it was not legal anywhere to procure a human body for study. The schools had to take it upon themselves to obtain these human bodies in illegal ways. The first way that they tried to accomplish this was by requiring the students to obtain the bodies themselves. It was illegal to steal a body, but the legal penalties were quite light. There were only fines to dissuade people from stealing bodies, but the populace of America had an entirely different idea of what the punishment for stealing bodies should be.

The general population of America felt that everyone deserved a proper burial after they died. Often, if someone was caught stealing a body from a grave, a lynch mob would capture that person and kill him. So while the legal penalties were by no means stiff, resurrectionists were always in fear of a lynch mob catching them.

The medical schools feared this as well. Sometimes the general population would break into the school and search for any human corpses. If they were to find any, they would destroy the school in which they found these bodies.

So the schools found that it was illogical to require their students to provide the bodies. This was not so much out of fear that the students would end up getting lynched. The schools were more afraid that the students would somehow botch the robbery and lead the mob to the school, and the school itself would suffer from the students' mistakes.

So the schools began to buy corpses through illegal channels. An entire group of professional resurrectionists grew out of this. In the 1800s, grave robbing had become an art. The robbers had tricks they could use that would assure that they would get away with this dark practice. They would often transport the bodies by train to different states so that the body could not be traced. They would steal the bodies from cemeteries, especially potter's fields. It was much less likely that the robbery would be noticed if the body was stolen from a cemetery than if it was stolen from a hospital or prison.

The medical schools themselves would apply methods that would assure that their use of the bodies would go unnoticed as well. They would have trapdoors and secret rooms in which they would hide the cadavers. That way, when the general populace would break into the school to try to find illegally obtained bodies, they would find nothing. By the 1800s, it was legal for many schools to use executed criminals in their medical studies, so the schools would oftentimes make the bodies unrecognizable before bringing them out for dissection. This way, if they were caught with the body, they could claim that the body was obtained legally.

Grave robbing became big business in America, and by 1878, the grave robbers had started to become a little sloppy.

Enter John Scott Harrison.

John Scott Harrison has the historical distinction of being the only man whose father and son were both presidents of the United States. His father was William Henry Harrison, and his son was Benjamin Harrison. He was also politically successful in his own right. He served as a congressman from Ohio from 1853 to 1857, some of the most turbulent years of the nation's history.

But John Scott Harrison is not really remembered for any of this. He is most clearly remembered for the events that occurred at Congress Green Cemetery in 1878.

In 1878, John Scott Harrison died at the age of 73. At the time, his son Benjamin Harrison was working in politics in Indiana. Benjamin Harrison came back into North Bend to attend to the burial of his father. John Scott Harrison's other son John Jr. was also there in North Bend to make sure all the arrangements were properly made for his father's burial.

The Harrisons had a family plot at Congress Green Cemetery. John Cleves Symmes was John Scott Harrison's grandfather, and there were still plots available for burials in and around the Symmes plot that were owned by the Harrisons.

When Benjamin and John Jr. arrived at Congress Green to pick out a burial location for their father, they were shocked to notice that there had been a grave on the other side of the cemetery that had been robbed. The body that was stolen was that of Augustus Devin, a cousin of John Jr. and Benjamin who had recently died. The resurrectionists had left the grave in a sad state of disrepair. It was obvious that it had been robbed; the grave had not even been filled back in after they took the body. Only the broken, empty coffin remained haphazardly tossed back into the hole.

Benjamin and John Jr. were quite distressed about this. They were worried because they figured that if grave robbers had robbed this grave, which lay just a short distance away from the family plot, what was to stop them from stealing the body of their father. The sons decided to employ drastic measures in order to assure that their father's body would not be stolen.

They decided to attack the problem from two different angles. First, they would bury their father in a secret grave site. They would leave no marker so that only the family would know the exact location where John Scott Harrison was buried. They were still afraid that this was not enough though. They were afraid that the fresh dirt would be discovered and that the grave robbers would still be able to find the grave. So as extra insurance against grave robbing, they decided to do the same thing that was done for Abraham Lincoln.

Soon after Lincoln's burial, grave robbers attempted to steal his body in order to hold it for ransom. They were caught, but Lincoln's body from that day forward was encased in an impenetrable concrete vault. Benjamin and John Jr. decided that they would enclose their father's body in a concrete vault in the secret location to assure themselves and their family that nothing would happen to the body of their father.

They completed the necessary arrangements and buried their father in Congress Green Cemetery, near the grave of John Cleves Symmes. Benjamin had to get back to important

This photograph depicts Congress Green Cemetery sometime near dusk. It was taken by Cincinnati Area Paranormal Existence Research (CAPER) as part of a training exercise for its new investigators. The stone box in the front left of the photograph behind the American flag is the final resting place of John Cleves Symmes, the founder of North Bend and cofounder of Cincinnati. The two headstones behind Symmes's grave are other members of the Harrison/Symmes family. A couple unusual images appear in this photograph. On the vertical headstones themselves, there appear to be two skulls imprinted on the stone. The photographer did not notice these images as the photograph was being taken. Also, there is an apparition behind a tree in the top right of the photograph. Are these tricks of the light, or are these images proof of the supernatural forces that walk this cemetery. (Courtesy of CAPER.)

matters in Indiana, but John Jr. decided that he would investigate the grave robbery of Augustus Devin that had occurred on the other side of the cemetery. He decided that he would feel better if these grave robbers that had desecrated the grave in his own family's cemetery were brought to justice. He wanted to make it clear that any robbery that occurred at Congress Green would be investigated to the fullest; he wanted the cemetery to be safe from all future robberies.

John Jr. went through days of thorough investigation of the crime. Throughout all these days of intensive investigation and questioning, he was able to trace the sale of the body to the Ohio Medical School in Cincinnati. He went to the school in order to ask school officials questions about where they attained their bodies. He was hoping to blow the whole black market scheme wide open. He was hoping to be a major player in the end of all grave robberies.

To his horror, when he walked into the school, he found the body of his father, John Scott Harrison, lying on a table. Despite all the effort that they had gone through to keep the body of their father safe, the robbers had somehow found the hidden grave and broken through the concrete vault. The body was ready for medical experimentation and dissection. It had been stored in brine during the last few days and moved with large sharp hooks.

John Jr. immediately retrieved his father's body from the school. The incident made headlines in all the papers around the country due to the fame of the body involved. Up to that point, the most famous stolen body ever discovered was that of Owen Brown, the son of the abolitionist John Brown. People were beginning to see how out of control the grave-robbing business was becoming.

The janitor at the medical school was implicated in the crime and forced to pay a fine, but the Harrisons and the citizens of Ohio did not feel that this was enough. The populace began to insist that the penalties for grave robbing become more severe.

That same year, a company in Columbus developed a grave-robbing deterrent. Essentially what it was was a bomb that would go off whenever a coffin was opened after burial. The era of grave robbers would not begin to come to an end, though, for another eight years. In 1886, two men murdered an old woman for the sole purpose of selling her body to a medical school. After this incident, grave robbing started a steep decline. While there may have been incidents as late as 1940, it would never again become as prevalent as it was in the 1870s and 1880s.

John Scott Harrison's body was reburied in Spring Grove Cemetery, a much more secure and guarded location. Eventually, his body would be moved into his father's grand tomb, which sits adjacent to Congress Green.

While perhaps the history of this terrible event is not apparent when one steps into the beauty of Congress Green Cemetery during daylight, once the sun dips below the horizon, those memories become all too apparent. It is during the night that the ghosts and the memories of Congress Green come out into the open.

The ghost stories that come out of this cemetery are vague at best. More often than not the sense that Congress Green is haunted is just that, a sense. No one can quite explain the feeling of unrest and discomfort they get sometimes when they are in the cemetery, but there are reports of people who get the sense that they are being watched. Sometimes people will even report light touches on their bare arms. Are these simply invisible strands of spiderwebs, or are these the spirits of those who are unable to rest here reaching out to touch the intruders?

Many times these vague reports of something not quite right at the cemetery even occur during the day. A group of ghost hunters from Cincinnati once went to the cemetery in order to try to catch a ghost. They got a photograph of a headstone with a strange spectral mist rising out of it, and a disembodied voice of a child became apparent when they wandered near the William Henry Harrison Tomb. Also, a photograph that they took appeared to show a soldier in Civil War era uniform. The misty photograph seemed to show a man holding a rifle with a bayonet at its end.

With such a dark history of grave robbery and tragedy, it is no surprise that stories of ghosts and spirits exist here. Perhaps the chills and discomfort that seem to follow one into the graveyard are malevolent spirits, plaguing the living. Perhaps it is almost in a sense of revenge, as it was only a little more than a century ago that the dead feared the living.

This photograph depicts the only cemetery in the village of North Bend. Today it is known as Congress Green Cemetery, but when North Bend's founder, John Cleves Symmes, first laid out the cemetery in the early 1800s it was known as the Pasture Graveyard. In 1814, Symmes himself was one of the first people to be buried in the cemetery. Over the years, many of North Bend's most prominent citizens were buried here in this cemetery. The cemetery gained national fame in 1878 when John Scott Harrison, the son of Pres. William Henry Harrison, was buried here at Congress Green. Shortly after his burial, his body was stolen from its grave and sold to the Ohio Medical School in Cincinnati for research purposes. His body was recovered before it was dissected. John Scott Harrison was reburied at Spring Grove Cemetery where it was considered safe from grave robbers.

Three

DELHI TOWNSHIP

Long ago, when pirates sailed around the oceans and seas creating carnage, they invented their own version of an afterlife. Since the pirates themselves felt that they were all far too evil to have any chance of entering the heaven that the Christians spoke about, they began to believe in an alternate heaven. They were not about to let the rest of the world tell them where they were going when they died.

In this heaven that the pirates imagined, this place where all sailors went when they died, there was a sense of eternal happiness. A fiddle would constantly play, and everyone would be constantly dancing and would never get tired. They called this version of heaven the Fiddler's Green.

Mount St. Joseph: Motherhouse and the Fiddler's Green

Today the Darby Lee Cemetery has almost been lost to history. It is nearly impossible to find. The easiest way to get there today is through the parking lot of a nursing home that sits off Bender Road in Delhi Township. If one were to park around the right side of the nursing facility, down the hill a little way there is a rusted sign that says, "Darby Lee Historic Cemetery." There is an arrow pointing into the woods.

One can tell that people do not often travel in these woods. The underbrush is thick. Only a small trail remains that leads back into the woods, but even this trail is overgrown with weeds and grasses. Spiderwebs crisscross the path at regular intervals. It is almost as if nature itself is protecting the small cemetery.

A dilapidated wooden fence sits between the path and the cemetery itself. It is a tiny cemetery as cemeteries go. It is maybe 20 feet across from corner to corner. The grass has overtaken the haphazard array of headstones. A couple of headstones are almost completely covered by grass. Almost symbolically, a single obelisk towers in the center of the cemetery, triumphing above the ravages of nature and time. It is a fitting tribute to the man who is buried underneath its impressive shadow.

In the mid-1800s, the land from near the bottom of Bender Road all the way up to where the Sisters of Charity Motherhouse and the College of Mount St. Joseph are belonged to a single farmer and his family. The farmer was caught up within a turbulent time in the nation's history, in one of the most turbulent places of that time.

In the mid-1800s, Ohio was a free state. It was illegal for anyone to own a slave in the state of Ohio. On top of this, many people in Ohio were becoming abolitionists. The entire state was beginning to realize the immorality of slavery and was strongly against it. Ohio became the first state that was governed by an abolitionist political party when Salmon P. Chase of the Republicans took the statehouse in 1856. Ohio also became a major stepping-stone in the Underground Railroad, since it bordered a slave state to the south. Throughout the history of the Underground Railroad, many slaves crossed the Ohio River from Kentucky to the freedom of the North.

This man's farm would become a sort of stepping-stone in the slaves' escape toward freedom. According to legend, the farmer was an abolitionist himself and worked hard to help the escaping slaves find their way to safety. His responsibility in aiding the slaves in their escape was making sure that it was safe to cross the Ohio River. If the farmer's sources told him that there were no slave hunters or law enforcement around on the river or on the way up to his home that night, the farmer would let the escaped slaves know that it was safe for them to cross. The slaves would then move into the relative safety of the farmer's home until it was safe for them to move farther north and toward Canada.

In order to escape detection, the slaves would often move only at night. On nights when it was safe to cross the river, in order to signal the slaves waiting in Kentucky, the farmer would light a lantern with green-tinted glass on the hill overlooking the river at the site where the cemetery sits today. He would light this green lantern and would play his fiddle. If the slaves saw the green light up on the hill and heard the fiddle music playing, they knew that it was safe to cross. If they waited in the thick woods of northern Kentucky and did not see the green light or hear the fiddle playing, they knew that it was not safe to cross that night.

The farmer was able to aid in the escape of countless slaves. After the Civil War ended and slavery was abolished throughout the country, the story of this farmer and his part in the Underground Railroad movement was celebrated throughout the city. There is a nearby street named Fiddler's Green, which could have been based on the story of this fiddler and his green lantern. The locals who still know the story call the Darby Lee Cemetery the Fiddler's Green Cemetery.

Eventually the fiddler died. He was buried on the site where he spent so many nights fighting for what he felt was right. His descendants would eventually sell the land and move away, but the fiddler himself will always be atop that hill overlooking the Ohio River.

As time passed, the stories faded and the old cemetery became lost in the woods. People stopped caring. Then people stopped knowing what had happened. Most people who live on the road called Fiddler's Green do not know the story anymore. The employees at the nearby nursing home do not know the story behind the man who is buried down that nearby overgrown trail.

While these employees do not know the story, they do often report strange things from back in the woods by the cemetery. The most commonly reported occurrences from those woods are strange green lights or the sound of fiddle music emanating from the cemetery.

Having heard stories of mysterious green lights in the cemetery, a curious teenager decided to check out the rumors for himself. He entered the forest down at the bottom of the hill by Route 50 and started the long hike up the overgrown path toward where the cemetery was. It was difficult travel. The path would almost disappear and be difficult to relocate from time to time since it had become so overgrown. Twice his flashlight went out for no reason and came back on after he shook it slightly.

Eventually, he began to near the cemetery and to his surprise he saw what looked like a dim green light in the forest up ahead. The light was so dim that he was not certain whether he was actually seeing a green light or if he was seeing some other light reflecting off green leaves. Whenever his flashlight was on, he could not see the light at all. When he stepped up to the cemetery, he turned off his flashlight so that he could look at the green light in more detail.

To his amazement, he saw a glowing green orb hovering about a meter above the ground. He circled the ball of light to assure himself that it was not simply an optical illusion. The ball of light appeared the same from all angles. He watched it for a few more minutes before it slowly dimmed to nothing. It vanished so gradually, it was almost as if it had never been there and had only been a trick of his eyes. Was this green orb a trick of the light or some optical illusion playing on his eyes, or was this the ghostly remains of the green lantern that led countless slaves up that hill to the safety of the farmhouse?

Not surprisingly, the strange glowing green light is oftentimes accompanied by the sounds of a fiddle playing in the distance. Once a couple decided to sit around in the cemetery at night to

This is a historic view of Darby Lee Historic Cemetery from the trail in the woods out toward the Ohio River overlook. While the cemetery may appear overgrown in this photograph, it is even more overgrown today. The tall monument in the picture is the headstone of Henry Darby. Henry Darby was an abolitionist who would oftentimes sit at this very site in the cemetery and let escaping slaves know that it was safe to cross the Ohio River. In order to alert them that the coast was clear, he would light a green lantern and play his fiddle. If the fugitive slaves saw the lantern and heard the music, they would know that it was safe for them to cross. To this day, people have reported seeing a green light and hearing fiddle music coming from this cemetery. (Courtesy of the Delhi Historical Society.)

Elizabeth Seton established the Sisters of Charity in 1809. In 1869, the Sisters of Charity moved into Delhi Township and bought the land known as Biggs Farm. They lived on the land for several years and then made plans to build the motherhouse there. This motherhouse would be the home of their charitable ministries and would replace the other two motherhouses in Cincinnati and Cedar Grove. Construction for this motherhouse began in 1882 under the direction of Mother Regina Mattingly. She died before the construction was completed and delayed the ultimate completion; however, they finished the construction in 1884 under the direction of Josephine Harvey. The building lasted one year before tragedy struck and the motherhouse burned down. Reconstruction began within the year, and a portion of the building was completed by 1886, allowing the Sisters of Charity to move back in and resume their work. (Courtesy of the Delhi Historical Society.)

see if they could witness this phenomenon that they had heard so much about. They wanted to actually see the green light and hear the fiddle playing. They sat there in the cemetery for about an hour when they both started to hear the sounds of music in the distance. It was too quiet to tell whether it was fiddle music or not. In fact, it sounded to them like it was coming from somewhere in the distance, not from the cemetery around them.

They figured that a car had parked somewhere with a window down and the radio up, or they were hearing the sounds of music from a nearby bar or party. They decided to try to find out where the sound was coming from, but the music seemed to get softer no matter which way they moved from the cemetery. It did not sound like it was coming from down the hill. It was not coming from down Bender Road, and it was not coming from the direction of the nursing home to the north. In fact, the music, as soft and distant as it sounded, was at its loudest within the cemetery itself. Perhaps it was the sounds of the farmer's fiddle reaching all the way into this world from beyond the grave.

As this abolitionist story began to fade into history, the farmland itself known as the Biggs Farm would take the history of the area in a different direction. In 1869, the Sisters of Charity would move onto the farm and take up their charitable ministries there.

Elizabeth Seton established the Sisters of Charity in 1809 in Maryland. Due to the charitable organizations she founded and the charity work that she herself did, Seton was the first person who was born in America to become a saint. The Sisters of Charity did work across the country and moved into the Cincinnati area in 1852. After building motherhouses in two different locations in Cincinnati, in the city itself in 1853 then in Cedar Grove in 1857, the sisters decided that they were going to move to a more permanent location in what is today Delhi Township.

In 1869, the sisters bought the Biggs Farm and lived there on the grounds for several years as the plans for a motherhouse on the site were established. Construction began in 1882 while the sisters were still under the direction of Mother Regina Mattingly. Unfortunately, before the building could be completed, Mother Mattingly suddenly passed away. She died before the motherhouse they had all been working so hard for was finished. She was one of the first sisters who were buried in what would become the Mount St. Joseph Cemetery. The cemetery sits just a short walk up a wooded path from the Darby Lee Cemetery.

In 1884, the Mount St. Joseph Motherhouse was finally completed for the Sisters of Charity of Cincinnati. Tragedy struck almost immediately after its completion, though. Within a year of the completion of the house, fire broke out in the building and spread quickly. Before anyone could do anything to save the structure, it burned to the ground; years of hard work became just smoldering wood piled on the ground. To add to the tragedy, several sisters became trapped within the structure as it burned and were unable to escape the burning building.

The tragedy of the fire was felt throughout the city, but the Sisters of Charity were soon able to get back on their feet and rebuild their razed motherhouse. Only one year later in 1886, Marian Hall was completed and the sisters were able to move back into the house.

When Mother Mattingly died unexpectedly in 1882, a woman named Josephine Harvey took over leadership of the sisters. Mother Harvey did not want the responsibility of mother, so after the sisters had settled into their new motherhouse in 1888, she resigned.

Mother Harvey was succeeded by a woman named Mary Hayes, but sudden tragedy would again strike the leader of the sisters. As plans were being made for new additions to the motherhouse in 1890, Mother Hayes suddenly died.

Construction would not begin on the center and east wings of the motherhouse until 1892, but finally the entire building as it stands today was completed. The finished building is a huge structure that overlooks the Ohio River off one of Delhi's hills.

In 1920, the Sisters of Charity would open up the first college for girls in Ohio called Mount St. Joseph. The college would operate within the expansive motherhouse complex until 1962,

In 1885, the Sisters of Charity's motherhouse burned to the ground. Most of the sisters were able to get out of the building before becoming trapped, but several sisters died in the fire. The fire started and spread too quickly for anyone to save the unfortunate women who were trapped in the building. Although a section was rebuilt within the next year, it was not until 1892 that the entire building was completed. Throughout this time, the motherhouse went through several changes. Mother Josephine Harvey resigned only six years after taking the position and was replaced by Mother Mary Hayes. Mother Hayes passed away shortly thereafter. In the early 1920s, the Sisters of Charity opened the doors to the first college for girls in Ohio called the College of Mount St. Joseph. The college was housed within the motherhouse until 1962, at which point it was moved to a tract of land adjacent to the motherhouse. (Courtesy of the Delhi Historical Society.)

when a new campus was built adjacent to the building. Today Mount St. Joseph College is a coed college with more than 2,300 students enrolled there. The Sisters of Charity still reside at the motherhouse complex, a witness to the building's rich history. The building is now a retirement center for the celibate nuns who have run Mount St. Joseph over the last 90 or so years.

According to many who have walked the halls of this building within the last 100 years, something else has taken residence there. People say that ghosts will often roam the halls of this expansive building.

Once a woman was walking the halls of the motherhouse after dark. She was alone. The long empty corridors and deafening silence enhanced this feeling of isolation. She began to feel uncomfortable. Chills started to crawl down her back, and the shadows around every corner began to frighten her. As she turned a corner, she saw a nun standing in the hallway.

She was immediately confused. The nun was not wearing what she should have been. Instead of wearing the elaborate black veil that a nun living in this building should have been wearing, the nun was wearing the traditional Mother Seton black cap. The Sisters of Charity had not worn the black cap as part of their dress code since the 1920s.

The nun stood motionless in the hallway as the woman slowly approached her. The oppressive feeling of loneliness and discomfort had not dissipated when she saw this nun. She still felt alone and felt as if something was wrong. She slowly approached the nun, and the nun quickly looked up at her. The nun's face was burned badly, as if she had been in a fire, and she had no eyes, just dark sockets where eyes had once been. In a panic, the woman screamed. As soon as she screamed, the nun vanished into thin air. Residents of the building ran to her aid to see what the problem was, but the apparition had vanished. The poor witness was trembling and alone in the hallway.

Oftentimes people will report seeing nuns walking the halls who simply vanish into thin air. On several different occasions people have reported seeing the apparition of Mother Regina Mattingly and Mother Mary Hayes walking the hallways. The witnesses are able to recognize them from old photographs and portraits that they have seen of these women.

Beyond these apparitions of nuns eternally walking the halls of the motherhouse, people have reported other paranormal happenings. Sometimes lights will flicker inexplicably when someone enters a room. Faucets will turn on by themselves. Doors will slam closed for no reason, and people will hear whispers coming from indiscernible sources.

The motherhouse complex is alive with activity, remnants of the blood, sweat, and tears that many generations of nuns had donated to its success. The grounds just opposite the motherhouse from Bender Road are now a large cemetery where only the Sisters of Charity can be buried. The grounds are beautifully landscaped and even retain this beauty within the grasp of the night. Not even the eeriness of the night can awaken the souls who sleep here.

And just down a heavily wooded path to the west, sometimes, when it is safe, a green light softly shines and beautiful fiddle music calmly plays.

Delhi Park: An Accidental Drowning

Delhi Park is a photograph of normality. The accessories of any park punctuate the fields. Everything seems well maintained by the township. The dried brown dirt of the baseball diamonds is kicked up by brief violent gusts of wind. Moonlight is sliced on this dirt by the metal cross-hatching of the backstop. Blue patches of light are traced by black shadows.

Almost randomly throughout the park, play areas for children are interspersed. Swings hang down from metal crossbars and are tossed around by unseen forces in the night. Metal slides accentuate the moon while plastic slides swallow it. Monkey bars, swinging bridges, and ladders fill in the play sets, waiting for morning when the children will come to utilize these metal and plastic toys.

Delhi Park sits between Foley Road and Delhi Pike. It has swings and slides for the kids, picnic tables and shelters for family picnics, and a skate park. There is a small pond just south of this fenced-in playground known as Clearview Lake. The lake sits behind an old bar known as Clearview Tavern. This lake is said to be the source of many of the ghostly sightings seen in this playground area. At least three people have died in this lake, and several children and locals have reported seeing men walking through this playground and vanishing mysteriously into thin air near the exits. In 2007, this playground area was torn down. Did this finally put these spirits to rest, or are the recent renovations only going to upset the spirits further?

On the south side of the playground just beyond the fence that determines the park's boundaries, there is a small lake known as Clearview Lake. On the other side of the lake is the Clearview Tavern. Clearview Lake has seen at least three fatalities, all of which were caused by drowning. The stories are unclear and vague. Once two men were swimming in the lake. Nothing unusual seemed to be happening until suddenly an unknown force pulled them both under the water. They fought to rise back to the surface, and they succeeded. After getting back to the shore, they heard the story of another man who had experienced the same thing and drowned in the lake due to the violent undertow. Another story tells of a man who killed himself in or near the lake. This suicide occurred within the past 10 years, so it is unlikely to be one of the spirits that roam the park today.

Deeper into the park, asphalt basketball courts are encaged in metal fencing. Some of the backboards are chipped; some of the rims are brown with rust.

From these basketball courts, the main access road to the park branches off two ways. To the south, the Delhi Public Library waits motionlessly. To the north the road is bracketed on either side by metal fences.

It is this part of the park, down the road to the north of the basketball courts, that houses the ghosts of Delhi Park.

Clearview Lake sits just outside the park, to the south of a metal fence. A fenced-in play area sits to the right. The lake is nestled within the woods. Trees surround it on all sides, and during the day people will often sit and fish along the small lake's calm shores. It belongs to the tavern that sits adjacent to the park. The tavern is called Clearview Tavern, and at one time it offered drinks and food to people who wanted to relax and fish at the lake.

The play area opposite the lake was once covered with all kinds of equipment. Several slides and swing sets were scattered across the fenced-in field along with a few other children's playthings. A huge picnic shelter decorated the center of the area. The slides and swing sets in this area were much older than any other recreational equipment in the park, and they were showing it. Rust was beginning to invade the edges of the equipment. All the other swing sets and slides throughout the park were constructed of more modern materials. Plastic and other corrosion-proof materials were used for those, but the playthings in this area seemed decrepit and more dangerous.

Recently the park removed everything from this area except for the huge wooden picnic shelter in the center. The area that for so many years had been a favorite place for children to play is now nothing but a fenced-in field. The ghost stories about Delhi Park all tend to begin in this now-abandoned area.

The legends of the place tell of two men who drowned in Clearview Lake. The stories are unclear about how the men drowned exactly. The stories only specify that they did in fact drown somewhere in that lake. These two men are the ghosts that haunt this park.

While there are no specific historic records that match this legend verbatim, there are similar historic stories that may have generated these tales. Once there were two men who were swimming in the lake. Unexpectedly they were both suddenly pulled under the water by some unseen force. Although they nearly drowned, they were able to struggle back to the surface and then back to the shore. When they got back to shore, they learned of the dangerous undertow that seems to sneak up on people and pull them under the water.

They learned that someone had drowned in the lake at one point in the lake's history for that very reason. He was surprised by the violent undertow in the small lake and was pulled underwater.

There was a second man who died in the lake. This man died under entirely different circumstances, and he died much more recently. The second man to drown in the lake decided that he was going to kill himself by drowning himself in the lake. He succeeded. Although this second man did die by suicide, it is unlikely that his spirit is one of the ones that is said to haunt the park. The suicide took place after the reports of the Delhi Park ghosts began.

The stories of how these two ghosts haunt the park are all eerily similar. Several different accounts tell of people who entered the park after dark and encountered these two men.

The first account involves two teenagers who entered the park after dark and began hanging out in the fenced-off play area across from the lake. They were startled to suddenly notice two grown men playing at the swings (the story occurred before the park removed the swings from the area) at the edge of the play area. The park was long closed, and the teenagers were trespassing in the park. They were surprised that there were others trespassing in the park, but they were more surprised that the trespassers seemed to be grown men.

As soon as the teenagers noticed these two men, the men started slowly walking toward the teenagers' position on the opposite side of the fenced-off area. The teenagers, concerned about their safety, started to move away from these two men and toward the exit of the park. The two men, their features and clothing both black in the darkness of the night, followed them all the way to the exit of the park. As the teenagers exited the park they looked back at the men who were chasing them. As soon as the teenagers stepped off park grounds, the shadowy men vanished into the darkness.

At least two other accounts tell of a similar encounter. Once a man driving his family through the area one night decided to take a shortcut by cutting through the park. The park connects Foley Road to Delhi Pike, and he thought it would be faster to cut through. It was past dark, but the gate was still open so he entered the park from Foley.

He slowly went over the speed bumps and saw two dark shadowy men in the fenced-off play area to his left. They both looked up at him and began to slowly walk toward the slow-moving vehicle. He was immediately frightened. He got a bad feeling from the two men, and he had his family in the car at the time. He decided that he would move through the park as quickly as he could to leave these two men behind.

It was not as easy to move quickly as he had thought. There were many sharp turns and skinny roads along the way. Speed bumps punctuated the road at about every possible spot.

He was able to climb the hill past the basketball courts at a rather fast pace, so he thought that he had left the two men far behind. When he glanced back behind him, though, he saw that the two shadowy men were right behind him, still walking slowly toward the car.

The father had no idea how they were keeping up. He began to fear that there were many groups of these dark shadowy people all throughout the park, but in the back of his head, he was convinced that they were the same two men from down at the fenced-in area.

He moved farther through the park, moving faster than he normally would have felt was safe. His wife asked him what was wrong since she had not seen the two men. He would not tell her though; he did not want to scare her or the children. Several more times as he sped ahead he looked back to see the two shadowy men still following close to him.

He breathed a sigh of relief as he exited the park near the McDonald's on Delhi Pike. As he entered these lights of civilization, the two shadows that had been following him vanished.

Other people have reported driving through the park late at night and seeing two indistinguishable men on those same swings or in the same area suddenly get up and start following them. This pursuit always continues until the moment when the trespassers leave the park. At this point those two men always disappear without a trace.

Are these two men just people who frequent the park after hours and follow others in an attempt to scare them away? Or are they the ghosts of those two unfortunate men who drowned on the outskirts of the park, come back to warn those who return to the site not to trespass on their eternal territory?

Sedamsville Woods: Man with the Bloody Axe

Fairbanks Avenue and Delhi Pike intersect at the northeastern corner of Sedamsville Woods. The woods are thick at this point; it is nearly impossible to see anything beyond the first line of trees, the sentinels that keep the evil of this place imprisoned in these cursed woods.

Rumors and legends abound; the woods are cursed, haunted by the memories and spirit of one of the most evil men to inhabit the west side of Cincinnati.

Legends say that something horrible happened in these woods long ago. A monster once lived in the woods, in an old house on a hill south of Delhi Pike. A small park at the intersection of Fairbanks Avenue and River Road sits at the base of the hill. The locals call it Sleeper's Hill.

In the mid-1900s, the people of Delhi generally stayed away from Sleeper's Hill. An old man owned the only house on the hill, and he pretty much kept to himself. He was a hermit of sorts, only rarely being seen by the other inhabitants of Delhi or the surrounding areas. This old man had acquired a strong sense of paranoia during his long secluded years on the hill. He figured that the residents of the town were out to get him, to destroy his property and to generally annoy him.

In retaliation against these imagined affronts against his property, the old man posted No Trespassing signs all along the borders of his property. He wanted to make certain that no one would set foot on Sleeper's Hill.

Most children from the town would stay far away from the hill. They were scared of the man who lived up there, and they heard lots of stories about how terrible he was and how violently he defended his property. Some children believed that he would stop at nothing to stop trespassing children; some said that he even killed to protect his house and barn at the top of the hill.

Children from the town would still wander off into the woods near the base of the hill. Some of the children had heard the rumors about the old hermit who lived in the house on the hill and decided that they would sneak up into the forest at night and pester the old man who lived up there. Other children would just be playing in the woods near the base of the hill, not really knowing about the paranoid man who lived at the summit, just trespassing obliviously in search of a more interesting playground.

When these trespassers would cross the line into his property there on Sleeper's Hill, many people from town would say that he would throw rock salt at the trespassers and chase them down the hill. Many times, "Old Man Sleeper" (the name the locals dubbed the man on the hill) would send his animals to chase after the trespassers as well. From time to time, kids who would wander up onto the hill would be chased by dogs or other animals from Old Man Sleeper's farm. Sometimes they were even chased by a bull that he would set free and send after the trespassing children.

While it probably actually happened historically that Old Man Sleeper would chase trespassers off his property with rock salt and his animals, more rumors would start to spread about him that seem to have no basis in historical fact. These rumors were probably spread because the locals were afraid to venture up onto the hill. The legends that people have come to believe are dark and terrifying.

Rumors started to spread that the man on the hill had started kidnapping children from town. Since his house was in the woods, out of earshot of civilization, he would take the children to his house where he would molest them in the solitude of his home. Then, to avoid discovery, he would kill the children and chop their bodies into small pieces with an axe. He would take these body parts and hide them around the woods during the night.

No evidence exists that supports these legends. No body parts were ever found in the woods, and missing children were never traced back to him. The rumors were probably spread around the town out of the hatred and fear of Old Man Sleeper.

By the end of the 1960s, another rumor started spreading through town among the younger residents of Delhi. It seemed that Old Man Sleeper had hung himself in the barn at the top of the hill.

The ghosts that haunt Sleeper's Hill seem to echo these stories.

In the 1970s, there was a group of men in their 20s who decided that they would go up onto Sleeper's Hill and set up a camp. It was a nice summer's night. They had set up the campground and had lit a fire. Sitting around the fire, they were talking to each other about everything and anything.

They stayed there long into the night, and they were still talking and having a good time at about 2:30 a.m. Suddenly a man who appeared to be about 70 years old walked by their camp.

Just south of the intersection of Fairbanks Avenue and Delhi Turnpike there is a small park at the foot of a rather large, heavily wooded hill. This unusual structure sits peacefully within the park. From 1950 to 1970, a series of rumors surfaced that the man who owned the land atop this hill would chase any trespasser out and throw rocks and other objects at them. Some area residents believed that he had a gun and would shoot the children if they crested the hill and stepped onto his farmland or would have the animals he kept on the farm chase the children away. The locals were terrified of this man, and most stayed far away from the hill. Local residents called him Old Man Sleeper. People who grew up in the area recount many incidents when they tried to climb the hill to Old Man Sleeper's place. Oftentimes they would be scared away.

Atop the hill where Old Man Sleeper lived, a body was found hanging in a shed. Many believe Old Man Sleeper killed himself there. In 1970, a man named George Korns and some of his buddies decided to camp out on Old Man Sleeper's farmland. By 1970, the land was nothing but a large clearing in the woods atop the hill. They had done this before and would always set up camp and sit around a fire telling ghost stories throughout the night. However, this night was a little different. As they were sitting around the fire, George noticed a man crest the hill. He was an older man, perhaps in his 70s, and he walked straight through the clearing. He stared straight ahead and walked without distraction. The man never looked over at George and never said a word. Eventually he vanished over the other side of the hill. George and his buddies were confused and did not know who it could have been. Was that Old Man Sleeper's ghost?

It was strange since it was 2:30 in the morning when the man walked by, but it was also very strange because the man did not look over at them. He had no expression and did not say a single word as he passed them and went over the other side of the hill. Perhaps the ghost of Old Man Sleeper was still roaming his beloved forested hill.

Other ghost stories about Sleeper's Hill are quite a bit scarier for those involved and seem to focus more on the rumors that Old Man Sleeper would kidnap children from town and kill them on the hill.

A teenager was roaming alone in Sedamsville Woods near Sleeper's Hill. Since the hill had gained a reputation for being haunted in town, some friends had dared him to wander the woods alone at night. In order to prove to them that he was not afraid of anything in those woods, he took a flashlight and hiked up into the woods in search of an old haunted house that was said to sit at the summit. These legends were probably all remnants of the man who lived there, and the house was probably his house, although it no longer stands at the summit.

The teenager roamed the woods and climbed the hill, trying in vain to find the abandoned house. Suddenly he heard people moving in the forest all around him. It was like there were people running past him. Whenever he would attempt to see these people with his flashlight, though, there would be nothing there.

Then he began hearing terrifying screams coming from all around him in the forest. He heard a distinctive scream coming from the south. When he shone his flashlight through the forest to try to see the source of the scream, another scream sounded from behind him to the north. The screams were realistic and seemed to be getting closer to him, so he switched off the flashlight so that he would not easily be spotted by whomever or whatever was screaming.

Eventually the screams seemed to be coming from right beside him, and he heard rustling from the underbrush right next to him. Then everything stopped. Everything went back to normal as quickly as it had begun. Unwilling to get caught up in whatever was happening again, the teenager rushed back to his friends to let them know what had happened. From the outskirts of the forest, they had heard no screams.

Other spirits that haunt the woods take on a much more sinister form. Once a group of teenagers went roaming through the forest in search of the infamous haunted house at the top of the hill. They too only carried flashlights with them as they penetrated the dark woods. When they reached the summit, they found a clearing. It seemed as if they were in a different world. They could no longer hear the cars passing on River Road just below the hill. No lights from civilization penetrated this far into the forest. The only light came from their flashlights.

They also noticed that it had gotten incredibly quiet. The crickets and forest sounds that had followed them throughout most of their adventure into the woods had stopped. The only sounds were their own voices and the leaves crackling underfoot.

As they were marveling at the seclusion of the place, they heard rustling coming from the edge of the clearing. Everyone looked out, expecting to see someone there.

Slowly, a man stepped out of the forest. He was holding an axe. The axe seemed to be dripping with blood. Everyone in the group ran down the hill. They scattered and ran headlong into the dark forest as the man with the bloody axe ran after them.

One girl got separated from the rest of the group, and the man started chasing after her. He was slowly advancing through the thick woods while she attempted to run. She would get tripped up often and fall flat on her face, having to pick herself up and grab her flashlight before she could continue to flee. The man was getting closer and closer to her, and just when she thought that he was going to catch up, she burst through the edge of the forest and onto River Road. She ran across the road in terror and collapsed on the other side, nervously looking back toward the woods.

No one emerged from the woods.

When she finally met up with the rest of the group, they all told the same story. They all said that the man with the axe had followed them alone down the hill. And then just when they thought they were caught, they burst through the edge of the woods, and the man did not follow.

People who roam the woods at night have repeatedly reported being chased back to civilization by a man with an axe. The man will appear out of nowhere and run after the unsuspecting witnesses with his infamous bloody axe, supposedly the same one that he used to chop up his victims during his life.

Perhaps the fact that the witnesses have never actually been caught makes the monster of these woods less frightening. At the same time, though, if these witnesses were caught, it would be unlikely that they would be able to return to civilization to report their experience. They would only join in the chorus of midnight screams that haunt this place at night.

Four

EDEN PARK

Is there a place beyond art, beyond beauty, beyond love, even beyond life? In the midst of the steel, the smog, and the noise of this city, nestled atop a hill and secluded from the downtown one can see in the distance sits a perfect little grove where not even the darkness can invade its serenity.

Eden Park: The Lady in Black

As Cincinnati's leaves turn from autumn gold to winter brown, Eden Park begins to look skeletal. Before the snows from the winter storms twinkle in the bright moonlight or the reflecting pool turns to crystal, the dying throes of October's wrath tear the last of the leaves from the crooked trees. The last leaf is dark and brittle as it is crushed underfoot. The tranquil outdoor paradise is vacant.

Eden's regular visitors let the park rest for the winter.

Just outside Eden's boundaries, life continues as normal. The cars and buses just down the street still run as regularly. People still walk, hurried, down the sidewalks, cigarettes hanging limply from their mouths. Everything except the weight of the people's coats seems the same.

Come mid-October, the road that climbs into the park feels a little more desolate, a little more alone.

The Cincinnati Art Museum towers to the south, its stone walls colder than to what they have become accustomed. A little farther east, the Playhouse in the Park and Mount Adams stand vigil, watching over the park while the ravages of winter take their annual toll. The setting sun always appears orange as it silhouettes the naked trees.

Once the sun dips below the horizon, the park is closed. An occasional car will traverse its winding streets, but the trails, the groves, the reflecting pool, and the 19th-century gazebo will not hear the reverberations of the living's footsteps until the sun rises again.

This gazebo's wooden structure punctuates a nearby winding intersection of roads. Many wooden pillars circle the structure, supporting the roof as it ascends to a point. A thick railing plays base to the pillars, and an opening breaks toward the road. Standing opposite the entrance, one can look out into the reflecting pool and beyond that to the skyline of the city itself. It is a quaint structure that remains as such despite its powerful visage and view.

Every so often, every few years, the green and white paint begins to chip and crack along the gazebo's body. Every few years the paint is retouched, leaving it to look as beautiful as it ever did. In fact, the gazebo is always being restored to its original facade. It never seems to change, staying constant despite the seasons.

Some say it is haunted.

Some say that despite the season, a dark resident lives in that structure.

This particular ghost has its origin in one of the most famous historical episodes in the history of Cincinnati. It is the story of George Remus.

George Remus was only five when he and his family moved to Chicago from Germany. He and his family would struggle throughout the early years of his life. When Remus was only 14, his father became disabled and was unable to work to support the family. Having no other options, Remus took a job at a local pharmacy and worked as hard as he could to support his family.

Over the next five years, Remus proved he was very good at the pharmacy business. Everyone who knew him knew that he was a very intelligent kid and would grow up to do great things. By the time Remus was 19, he was able to purchase the pharmacy where he worked. Over the next couple of years, he was able to buy out several more pharmacies in the area. By the time he was 24, Remus owned a little pharmacy empire within the city of Chicago.

But he soon grew tired of the pharmacy business and decided that he would become a lawyer. Since he was so intelligent, becoming a lawyer was not a problem for him, and he was soon making more money as a lawyer than he was at his pharmacy empire.

Remus made his living as a criminal defense lawyer, defending some of the worst criminals to pass through the courts in Chicago. Murderers and thieves would often be acquitted through his defense. Things were going very well for Remus, and over the next few years they would only get better.

When 1920 came around, Remus's place in history would change forever. By the time Prohibition started in 1920, Remus had divorced his wife in order to marry his secretary and mistress Imogene. He also decided that bootlegging would be a very profitable business to get into. Many of his clients were into the bootlegging scene and seemed to have incredibly large amounts of money as a result. Remus figured that bootlegging was the way to great fortune and decided to get involved.

Remus spent months studying every aspect of the Volstead Act and eventually figured out loopholes in the Prohibition laws. Apparently, with his pharmacy business, Remus could purchase whiskey from legal distilleries for medicinal purposes. His plan was to purchase his alcohol through these legal channels and then "steal" his own shipment of whiskey to sell to underground bars.

Remus decided to headquarter his bootlegging business in Cincinnati since it was geographically central to 80 percent of the legal distilleries in the country. His plan and his business sense made this illegal venture a huge success. In order to stay out of trouble, he would bribe city officials to turn a blind eye on his illegal activities.

By the end of 1922, Remus had made more than $40 million. He owned a huge mansion named the Marble Palace in the Price Hill suburb of Cincinnati and would often hold huge parties for the elite of the city. The most famous of these parties was the 1923 New Year's party that he held. He invited 100 of the most powerful people in the city to the party and presented every man who attended with a diamond-studded watch and every female who attended with a brand-new car. Remus quickly gained a reputation for being very generous with his money. He was a figure who was respected throughout the city despite the dark means by which he made his money.

Things began to fall apart for George Remus in 1924 when the government began to come down hard on bootlegging across the country. Remus was convicted of violating Prohibition laws and was sent to the Atlanta Federal Penitentiary for two years.

The Atlanta Federal Penitentiary was not a very bad place to be for an inmate with the money that Remus had. He and many of the wealthy inmates there were able to bribe the warden, Albert Sartain, to treat them well. They would get private cells and nice meals while the rest of the inmates would be stuck with roommates and prison food. No one in the prison would mess with Remus because the prison guards were constantly protecting him.

In order to make sure that his financial empire continued to run smoothly in his absence, he gave Imogene power of attorney over his money. He felt he did not have much to worry about while he waited for his time to be up. He was looking forward to returning to his mansion in Cincinnati.

While he was in prison, Remus met another inmate named Frank Dodge, and they became quick friends. Remus told him about how his wife had control of all his money and other secrets

George Remus was born in Germany in 1876 and moved to Chicago almost five years later. At the time of this 1918 photograph, Remus resided in Chicago. This photograph shows him (left), his sister Elizabeth Remus Dobbratz (standing, right), his mother Marie Remus (sitting, right), and his nephew Elroy Dobbratz (front, right) standing next to his father's grave. Not long before his father passed away, he took over the pharmacy business that his father had run. Soon though, George Remus tired of the pharmacy business and decided to pursue other interests. He decided to use the money that he had acquired through his pharmacy to put himself through law school. Two years after the death of his father, George Remus moved to Ohio and continued his law practice and studies. His study of the law and his understanding of the pharmaceutical business would be instrumental when he decided to delve into bootlegging. (Courtesy of the Delhi Historical Society.)

Eden Park is a beautiful park that sits atop Mount Adams. From Eden Park, there are many spectacular views of downtown Cincinnati and the surrounding areas. This gazebo sits in the center of the park near a large reflecting pool. Perhaps the most famous murder that Cincinnati has ever seen happened here at this gazebo. When George Remus was released from prison, he discovered that his wife had been having an affair. She soon filed for a divorce. His chauffeur drove him to the court hearing while his wife Imogene rode in a taxi. George saw Imogene's taxi ahead of him as he rode through Eden Park near this gazebo. He told his chauffeur to run her off the road. George got out of the car and began yelling and screaming at Imogene. The argument escalated, and George took out a gun and shot Imogene. She died at this gazebo wearing a black dress.

about his life. Unfortunately, Dodge was actually an FBI agent who was working undercover in the prison to expose the warden for taking bribes from the inmates. Dodge finished his investigation and got out of the prison long before Remus.

Almost as soon as Dodge left the prison, he resigned from the FBI and went to find Imogene in Cincinnati. Dodge and Imogene began having an affair, and soon Dodge convinced her to take all Remus's money. Imogene sold the distilleries that Remus owned and started hiding all his assets that she could liquidate so that he could not get at it when he was released from prison.

In order to secure their own safety once Remus got out of prison, Dodge and Imogene tried to get rid of him. First they tried to have him deported, claiming that when his father moved to Chicago from Germany, he never became a U.S. citizen. When that did not work, they tried to pay a hit man $15,000 to kill Remus. This strategy also failed.

Dodge and Imogene went into hiding when Remus was released from prison. Eventually, though, Imogene wanted to marry Dodge, but in order to do that, she had to first divorce Remus. The divorce was a messy one that had to go to court.

On the last day of the divorce hearing, when the divorce was going to be finalized, Imogene took a cab to the courthouse. She wore a black dress to mourn the loss of the marriage. Remus was being driven to the courthouse by chauffeur, and he happened to see Imogene in the cab as they neared Eden Park.

Remus had his chauffeur run the taxi off the road. Both vehicles came to a stop in front of the gazebo in Eden Park. Remus and Imogene jumped out of the vehicles and started yelling at each other in broad daylight in front of everyone who was at the park that day. Suddenly, without warning, Remus took out a gun and shot Imogene in the abdomen. She crumpled to the ground and died there in front of the gazebo wearing her black dress.

Remus was suddenly caught up in a media frenzy that followed him to the courthouse. He was going to be tried for the murder of Imogene. With so many witnesses and a clear motive, the prosecution felt it had an easy case on its hands. Remus would quickly prove them wrong. Against the suggestion of the judge, Remus decided to represent himself in the case due to his criminal defense background.

Again, Remus had the chance to comb through the law and find a loophole that he could try to slip through. He did. He plead temporary insanity, a plea that was unheard of in that time.

Throughout the trial, he would demonize Dodge and Imogene. After all, they had had an affair behind his back and had attempted to take all his money. The jury deliberated for less than 20 minutes before acquitting Remus by reason of temporary insanity.

Unwilling to let him get away with murder, the prosecution attempted to have him committed to a mental asylum since he had been found insane. During that trial, the prosecution sabotaged itself. In the original trial, the prosecution called many psychologists as witnesses who claimed that Remus was not insane. He simply used the prosecution's own evidence against it and got out of serving time in a mental asylum.

Remus had gotten away with murder. Since he had been in prison, bootlegging had become a much more violent business, so Remus took the money that he had already made and left the business. He moved to a house across the Ohio River in Covington where he lived for the next 25 years in relative anonymity. He died in 1952.

It is not the ghost of George Remus, though, who still haunts Eden Park. It is the ghost of Imogene.

This haunting is different from most. When speaking of haunted places, a myriad of strange occurrences seem to envelop most places. One will often hear of disembodied voices from impossible sources, phantom footsteps that echo what once walked there, distant sounds of screaming or of children playing, and feelings of uneasiness and chills that crawl through one's skin.

Only one ghost haunts this place. Only one supernatural resident walks this park after the sun dips below the horizon and the orange twilight punctuates those late-autumn nights.

She is the lady in black.

Since the ghost is always seen wearing a black dress, it is only logical to conclude that the woman is the ghost of Imogene Remus. She was murdered by her husband in cold blood in front of the gazebo. She was murdered in a black dress.

Legends say she still wears that dress today.

A man was walking his dog around the adjacent reflecting pool at dusk one night. As the sun went down, all the shapes and landmarks of the park slowly began to lose their definition. Everything was lost in an orange haze.

When the man turned to walk back toward the gazebo, he noticed that there was a silhouette of a woman standing in the gazebo, looking out toward him and his dog. Due to the poor lighting conditions, the man could not see any definition to her, just that she was a woman in a black dress. At first he was not even certain that there was anyone there. He thought that his eyes could have been tricking him. He thought that perhaps the pillars of the gazebo were playing with his vision, casting shadows from the setting sun and streetlights.

As he came closer and closer to the gazebo, he was certain that there was a woman looking out over the reflecting pool. He noticed that she was no longer looking at him but was gazing absently out to the area where he was when he first noticed her. Even as he walked up the sidewalk adjacent to the gazebo, he was unable to see any detail in her face. She was still looking out across the reflecting pool, but she looked like she was just a solid shadow.

As he rounded the corner by the road, he decided that he was going to approach the woman in the gazebo since her appearance had been so surreal throughout his ordeal with her. He walked around the corner but lost sight of her for a second. The sidewalk he was walking on passed underneath the gazebo, and some tall bushes blocked his sight lines.

When he turned the corner to where he could see into the gazebo again, it was empty. There was no one there, and he saw no one walking away. He had only lost sight of her for a second, yet she had vanished without a trace.

He was not the only one to witness this apparition in or around the gazebo. Sightings of the mysterious lady in black happen often. Since the park officially closes after dark, many of the sightings are made by passing cars or by people just passing through at twilight. The accounts are often very similar though. A woman in black is seen in or near the gazebo, and she is just staring absently at something. She never seems to notice anyone who sees her, and when the witnesses approach her, she vanishes without a trace. The people who see her wonder if she was ever there or if she was just a trick of the lighting.

The ghost is shy. There are no accounts of her ever speaking. No disembodied voices travel through the gazebo; no one claims to hear distant screams. The ghost simply appears, perhaps to again admire the view, perhaps replaying those last moments of her short life.

The Cincinnati Art Museum: The Mummy's Specter

In 1881, the citizens of Cincinnati felt that they needed some way to bring more culture and beauty into their city. After a successful museum of art was established in Philadelphia in 1876, Cincinnati decided that it would build an art museum of its own. By 1885, the first building in the Cincinnati Art Museum was constructed in Eden Park near Mount Adams. It was built on a hill that overlooked the skyline of the city itself, surrounded by the beauty of nature.

It was the first art museum built west of the Appalachian Mountains, and as soon as it opened, it was known throughout the region as the "Art Palace of the West." Today a driveway ascends from the main road in the park up past a magnificent overview of the skyline of the

Since the Cincinnati Art Museum was built over a great many years, the building's exterior has taken on a similar eclectic tone to the interior. Usually these additions are created with entirely different architects and artistic visions. While the front of the building takes on a more Greek or Roman style with its massive pillars and gray stone facade, this section of the building seems to be completely different. This section of the museum was the original art museum before any of the additions or wings were added. Its brownstone exterior and medieval castlelike appearance create a sharp contrast to many of the other wings of the building.

In 1881, citizens in Cincinnati made plans to build an art museum. It would be the first art museum built on the west side of the Appalachian Mountains. It was built on Mount Adams just up a small hill from Eden Park. The museum looks into the beautiful park below and toward the magnificent Cincinnati skyline. By 1885, the first section of the museum was completed. Construction continued for the next 50 years, adding a new wing in 1907 and the final two in the 1930s. In the end, the building became be a large rectangle with a courtyard in the center. After all the construction was completed, the interior became a maze of corridors and large rooms ideal for the Cincinnati Art Museum and its enormous art collection.

city itself. The trees step aside, allowing this breathtaking view of the city below. The energy and dynamics of the buildings and streets are visible from the quiet tranquility of Eden Park.

Up the driveway farther, the museum appears to be several completely different buildings that somehow connect into a maze of corridors and floors. The first part that one comes to when climbing the drive appears to be some kind of nondescript gray dormitory of sorts. The walls are flat and plain, punctuated only by regular windows lining each floor. The next style of architecture that one comes upon is along the driveway in the middle of the building. There is an entrance here but not the main entrance that is meant for public use—it is an entrance to a school and for staff. This section of the building appears creepy. The walls are made from old brownstone, and the door and windows have a more medieval feel. Finally one rounds the corner to the public lot where the main entrance to the museum sits. Here the architecture is more Roman with huge stone columns playing sentinel at the entrance.

This eclectic array of architectural styles is due to the several additions that expanded the museum over its 125-year history. In 1907, another wing was added to the original 1885 structure. Then in the 1930s, two more wings were added to the building, enclosing the structure in a rectangle. In the center of the art museum complex is a courtyard that has been created through these building projects.

Inside the building, corridors seem to intertwine with one another forever with no real discernable beginning point or ending point. Art from most every period rests somewhere within these walls, from ancient Greek and Egyptian sculpture to Andy Warhol's pop art to modern multimedia works of art that were created in the last couple years. At more than 60,000 works of art, the museum holds more art than any building in the state of Ohio.

The hallways all have a feel of sterility, and the building itself seems to echo. The floors are largely uncarpeted, and any furniture is without cushions. The hallways and rooms are all quite large but only rarely have anything in the middle of the room. The large barren wooden and marble floors are mostly empty. Only the displayed artwork decorates the walls.

Soon after one enters the massive front doors to the building, the Egyptian, Greek, and Roman section of the museum stretches down a hallway ahead. Here there is an actual dead body, the mummified remains of some ancient Egyptian man. This body is not said to be the source of the art museum's ghost though. The ghost resides just beyond the mummy, in another ancient Egyptian artifact.

A sarcophagus.

The museum purchased the sarcophagus in 1976, and it sat in storage for nearly a decade after that. Nothing strange seemed to happen with the item while it sat hidden in storage for all those years. When the sarcophagus was placed on display in the 1980s, though, people began reporting strange occurrences that would often be centered around this ancient coffin.

Several different sources have reported very similar sightings of this particular ghost. Witnesses see a black cloud of smoke slowly rise above the sarcophagus. This black cloud of smoke will hover for several moments above the sarcophagus before rising farther and disappearing into the ceiling. This featureless specter has appeared on several occasions and always disappears through the ceiling without interaction with those witnessing it.

A storage room is directly above where the sarcophagus sits. Oftentimes security guards will take naps in this storage room during their breaks or when nothing is going on. Once a guard decided to take a nap in this security room during one of his breaks. As he was drifting off to sleep, he was suddenly filled with a sense of fear and dread. He felt that something was wrong. When he opened his eyes, he saw a terrifying floating face hovering right in front of him. The guard panicked and tried to get around the face to the exit of the storage room. The face floated into his way, blocking his escape for several horrifying minutes. Eventually the face simply dissipated and the guard was allowed to escape unharmed.

Many other guards have had unsettling experiences in this storage room. Another guard had walked into the storage room and immediately felt very uneasy. As he walked to the other end of the room, he heard footsteps in the room but could not find anyone there. He would hear the door creaking open and closed, but he could see that it was not actually moving. Frightened, the guard started to walk toward the door to get out of the room, and he heard a whisper behind him. He said that the whisper sounded like it was spoken in a different language that the guard did not recognize.

Another story that circulates among the employees at the art museum involves a suicide that is rumored to have occurred on the top floor of the museum. The top floor exhibits works of modern art. An overlook in the center of the floor looks down through all the other levels of the museum. Rumor among some employees is that a man hung himself from the top floor. He tied the noose around his neck and jumped over the overlook. He slowly strangled to death as he dangled above the museum.

His ghost is also said to haunt the museum sometimes after dark.

Once a gift shop employee was closing down the store for the night. He decided to go through the main room to use the restroom before going home. As he was entering the room, he heard some commotion on the top floor of the building. As he slowly entered the main room, he saw swinging shadows being cast across the walls. The shadows looked like someone had hung himself. He quickly looked up, expecting to see someone swinging from the top floor overlook, but there was nothing there.

The building is large and filled with long echoing corridors. Footsteps and shadows from across the building can sound as if they are near as one walks the endless corridors. Perhaps tricks of the acoustics or shadows of unusual sculptures can explain away some of the strange things that seem to happen throughout the building. But echoes in the building cannot fully explain the figures and specters that have been seen near the sarcophagus display. Perhaps they can be explained away as figments of those witnesses' imaginations, or perhaps the ghost of the human who was laid to rest in that sarcophagus is upset at being moved away from his home, halfway across the world, to Cincinnati.

Five

EZZARD CHARLES DRIVE

Immune, invisible, untouchable. It seems improbable that places like this exist. But they do. There are places that stand cold against a firestorm, that stand still amid an earthquake. Sometimes in the most economically crippled parts of town, the most vandalized, among the crumbling stone, lost vagrants, and garbage-lined streets, there stands an anomaly: an untouched structure of aesthetic masterwork, geometric lines where poverty stops and beauty prevails. Do the forces of decay respect these masterpieces or fear them?

Music Hall: Unconsecrated Ground
All night long, every night, a ghost light burns onstage at Music Hall. It is considered good luck, perhaps a needed touch of illumination so that the ghosts can continue to perform and watch long after the building's living element has left for the night. The ghost light is just a single bulb, hardly affording any light to many of the dark corners of the main stage, but ghosts have never needed much light.

Ghosts tend to haunt the unseen corners of the world, only glimpsed occasionally by those lucky (or perhaps unlucky) enough to encounter them—encounter that brief connection between the world of the living and the world of the dead.

Music Hall is colossal. It takes up two city blocks between Eleventh and Thirteenth Streets. Inside, it twists around like a labyrinth. Stages, ballrooms, lounges, dressing rooms, and offices twist around endlessly. Remote staircases and hallways are blocked off and used for storage, but these passages are so remote that they seem to be better used as storage than as a path from one place to another.

A huge, warehouselike room is used to build props for the stage. A similar room is used for painting these props. The critics have a lounge for relaxing before and after performances. The performers have dressing rooms and lounges of their own as well as a practice room that mirrors the main stage.

The building stretches on and on, a new, functional room around every corner.

Ghosts live here. They co-inhabit the building peacefully with the living element. The ghosts seem to run the building after hours or in the quieter, less hectic times while the living run the building during business hours and during the crowded evening performances. The building is never completely silent and empty. There is always something happening within the myriad corridors of Music Hall.

The story that is perhaps most frequently reported about this building involves the freight elevator. In order to operate the freight elevator, one needs a special key. Without the key, the elevator will not work. Despite this, the elevator will oftentimes come on by itself and will move from floor to floor without anyone turning it on with the key.

Once an employee at Music Hall decided that he was going to ride the freight elevator from the third floor all the way down to the bottom floor of the building. As he stepped into the elevator and began to ride it down, he began hearing soft whispering coming from all around him in the elevator despite the fact that he was alone. As he rode farther on the elevator, the whispers got angrier and angrier until it seemed as if these phantom voices were yelling at him.

The message was clear; they wanted him out of the elevator. When the elevator finally stopped at the bottom floor and the door opened, the employee was happy to oblige.

Employees tend to experience many strange things within these walls. Oftentimes they will report seeing figures dressed in 19th-century dress walking down hallways or standing in the auditoriums. No one is ever able to get close enough to any of them to speak to them, and the security tapes show that no one is there, only an empty hallway or an empty auditorium.

Night security guards, locking up and doing one last sweep of the building, also have many stories about strange happenings in Music Hall. Security will sometimes report strange sounds or voices. A guard heard laughter coming from one of the auditoriums but upon investigation, found the room empty.

Another guard tells the story that as he was locking up one night, he heard footsteps following him all throughout the building. Once he heard a door that he had just finished locking open up and slam shut behind him. Upon investigating the door, he discovered that it was still locked and secure.

People will report strange sounds coming from all over the building, a woman's voice singing beautifully from an empty auditorium, and distant conversations going on within the locked building.

Music Hall is haunted. It is perhaps the most famous haunted place in the city of Cincinnati. Perhaps the dead are forever lost in its endless maze of corridors and rooms. Perhaps they never want to find their way out.

While it is commonplace for theaters to be considered haunted, perhaps by patrons and performers who have spent the greatest years of their lives within the theatrical walls, the haunted history of Music Hall seems to trace its origin to the site where it was built. Granted, some of the ghost stories of this building could very well be the spirit of a singer returning to sing one last song or deceased patrons chatting as they get lost within the corridors, but there is a darker history that surrounds the site where Music Hall was built.

Three historical places are reputed to have existed on the site where Music Hall now sits. Any one of the three would be reason enough for the building to be haunted.

First, the site may have been the location of the city's first hospital. It was called the pesthouse and was used to treat patients who were suffering from the cholera epidemic in the mid-1800s. There was no cure for the dreaded disease, so the hospital was mostly intended to both separate the patients from the general population and to make them as comfortable as possible as they died. It is now generally accepted by historians that the pesthouse did not actually sit on the site that is now Music Hall. Back in the 1800s, the road that passes Music Hall on the western edge, Central Parkway, was actually a canal. The pesthouse probably sat on the western side of the canal, opposite where Music Hall sits today. Still, the pain and suffering that occurred there must have been unimaginable, and its proximity to the modern Music Hall cannot be forgotten as a possible cause of some of the hauntings.

Next, the place where Music Hall now sits was originally the site of an orphan asylum that housed more than 70 abandoned children. Conditions in buildings such as this were deplorable in the 1800s. Budgets were low for the orphans, and proper care and food were impossible to afford.

Because of improper supervision, several children died as a result of falling into the canal while playing near its eastern bank. Since these children never learned how to swim, they drowned there as their friends watched helplessly.

In 1861, when the Civil War began, the orphanage moved to Mount Auburn. Seventeen years later, in 1878, architect Samuel Hannaford built the Gothic-style Music Hall on the orphan asylum's wire frame supports. Backstage, where the lighting rigs and scenery suspension are built, one can still see the wire frame structure and foundation from the original 1850s orphan asylum.

Music Hall contains much more than simply an auditorium. On the second floor of the building, there is a large ballroom, used as a venue for proms and other large events. In a hidden corner of this ballroom, there is a freight elevator. This freight elevator is reputed to be the most haunted location in the building. The elevator is near the south side of the building, which was once a pauper's graveyard before Music Hall was constructed. During recent renovations to the elevator, human remains were discovered in the elevator shaft, most likely remnants of that potter's field. The elevator itself does not work like a standard elevator. A key is required in order to summon the elevator to one's floor. Sometimes, though, the elevator will inexplicably rise to certain floors without a key. Also, threatening voices are often heard within the elevator.

Music Hall is a huge building that stretches two city blocks from Eleventh Street to Thirteenth Street. The structure was built as a meeting place for large crowds. Those who originally conceived this project hoped that the building would not only be used for performances but hoped that it would be used for any large exposition that came into town. It eventually became the home of the Cincinnati Symphony and the Cincinnati Opera. At the time the building was completed in 1878, many patrons would either arrive by carriage on Elm Street or would arrive by boat on the canal side (today Central Parkway). The canal was drained and paved over almost a century ago, but the Elm Street side of Music Hall still appears much the same as it did in the late 1800s. This photograph shows Music Hall from the Elm Street side.

Perhaps the children who died within those walls or within the adjacent canal still haunt the maze of corridors and auditoriums.

Also near the south end of where Music Hall now sits was the site of an old potter's field. In the 1800s, cemeteries were designated by the faith of those buried there. There were Catholic cemeteries, Baptist cemeteries, Jewish cemeteries, and many more. The place where one was buried was based on what church or synagogue one frequented.

If people died and could not afford to be buried in their particular faith's graveyard, or if the deceased had committed suicide or had committed some other mortal sin that excluded them from being buried in consecrated ground, then their bodies would be quickly disposed of in a potter's field. It was generally accepted by the religions of the day that if people were not buried in consecrated ground, they would be damned to hell for all eternity. Many times, the graves in a potter's field would not even be marked so the identities of those buried there were soon lost to history.

When Music Hall was built on the site in 1878, the potter's field had to be moved to make way for the magnificent structure. Unfortunately, it seems that moving the graveyard elsewhere was not as easy a task as everyone had hoped. Since many of the graves were unmarked, many bodies remained in the field and were covered by the foundations of Music Hall itself.

Recently, when renovations were being done on the south side of the building, construction workers were digging out the bottom of the freight elevator shaft. As they were doing this, they began to discover human remains. At first they assumed that the remains were those of homeless people who became trapped in the shaft, but upon further study it was discovered that the bones were much older than this. The bones were more likely remains of people who had been buried in the potter's field.

In 1884, one of the most deadly riots in the history of America had its origin at Music Hall. Two men were accused of having murdered their employer in order to rob him. One of the two murderers, William Berger, was able to hire a high-profile lawyer and was only convicted of manslaughter, an offense that did not merit hanging for punishment.

The citizens of Cincinnati were outraged. They felt that the jury had been bribed, and they felt that Berger deserved to hang like any other murderer of the day. A group of 10,000 protesters gathered at Music Hall to decide what they were going to do about it. They decided that they would march on the courthouse and hang Berger themselves.

The mob attacked the courthouse and killed all the murderers that were being held there. Berger had been shipped out of town to Dayton already, so he was no longer in the courthouse. Furious, the rioters burned the courthouse to the ground and attacked police and government officials who approached them. The mob held control of the city between Music Hall and the courthouse.

Eventually the National Guard was called, and it was able to disperse the mob. All told, about 56 people were killed in the riots, making it the bloodiest riot in Ohio's history. Perhaps remnants of this riot still haunt Music Hall, the meeting place and origin of the event.

Where the ghosts of Music Hall came from is ultimately unimportant. What is important is that somewhere within these rooms and auditoriums, spirits from another time still roam. Some are angry. Some are not. Some walk endlessly, their footsteps forever echoing these endless corridors.

Cincinnati Union Terminal: Tragic Reminiscence

Standing on the front steps of the Cincinnati Union Terminal, one can see Music Hall looming powerfully down the road. A little farther and to the right, the setting sun silhouettes the skyline of Cincinnati. Looking out toward the city from these front steps, most of the magnificent architecture of southwest Ohio is presented.

Inside Music Hall there are a great deal of rooms including a ballroom, a critics' lounge, offices, dressing rooms, an expansive basement, and set construction rooms. However, the most famous room in Music Hall is depicted here. It is called Springer Auditorium. Springer Auditorium is known for its excellent acoustics. Sound will travel equally well to every one of the 3,630 available seats. Another defining feature in the auditorium is the two-ton chandelier that hangs from the center of the domed ceiling. The auditorium is home to the Cincinnati Symphony every year. It also houses the Cincinnati Opera, the Nutcracker production, and many other events. Behind the stage of the Springer Auditorium, a large 90-ton steel grid framework supports the scenery, sets, and lighting. This large grid is the same steel grid that once supported the orphan asylum structure in 1844.

Arguably, though, the greatest work of architecture in Cincinnati is right behind. The Cincinnati Union Terminal is unique in its magnificence. Exteriorly, its dome towers, impossibly high, swallow the remainder of the sky. The huge clock on its face keeps constant time; trains never seem to be late. When it was constructed in 1933, it was the only half dome in the western hemisphere and was the largest half dome in the world.

Outside, there are two walking tunnels on each side of the building, leading down to the street next to the lot. These tunnels were gated off and closed down long ago, just a reminder of when this building used to be a functioning transportation center for the city. These tunnels would take passengers from the front of the terminal, down into the outskirts of the city itself. Sometimes one can hear children's laughter emanating from those tunnels, although the rusted gating will not allow even small children to enter these short, dark tunnels.

Inside the massive half dome of the main concourse itself, despite any hustle or bustle one might encounter, the acoustics will carry a whisper from one corner to the other. It seems impossible. A scream will barely carry from the middle of the massive room to one of the sides, but the perfectly curved walls will guide the sound of a whisper from one side to the other.

In 1890, Cincinnati was a major hub of transportation in the Midwest. Seven different major train companies had terminals dispersed throughout the city. Since rail was the primary way that anyone in the 1800s would move about the country, it was likely that someone traveling through the Midwest would end up in Cincinnati at one point or another.

While there were many trains that moved constantly through Cincinnati, the organization of the whole system was somewhat lacking. If a passenger was heading to a certain destination, it was possible that the passenger would have to pick up a connecting train when he reached Cincinnati. If the connecting train was with the same rail company, this was not a problem. Oftentimes, though, passengers would have to catch connecting trains from different rail companies, and this often meant that the passengers would have to find some way to cross the city and find the other rail terminal before they missed their connection.

The City of Cincinnati knew that something had to be done about this and in 1913, plans were started to build a union terminal. This terminal would house all the city's major rail lines so that passengers would not have to worry about traveling across town to catch their connecting trains.

The city created the Union Terminal Company, whose sole purpose was to design and build the terminal that would bring all the city's railroads together. Mayor Russell Wilson laid the cornerstone of the building in 1931, and the entire project was completed just two years later in 1933.

When it finally opened, it was a huge transportation center in the city. Every day, 216 trains would pass through the gigantic terminal and countless passengers would move on to other cities throughout the country. In the midst of the Depression and with the rise of streetcars and automobiles, the popularity of train travel began to quickly wane. By the end of the 1930s, the terminal was already being called a waste of money and resources that the city could have otherwise used.

The terminal picked up in popularity again in the 1940s with the outbreak of World War II. People going off and coming home from war would ride the countless trains that took them to their destinations. Many people saw their families for the final time here within these walls as they waved their good-byes before going off to war. Others experienced their most joyous reunions at this station as they returned from the war to families that were never certain that they would see their beloved soldiers again.

But after the war ended, the popularity of the train terminal declined quickly. Many of the rail companies went out of business and pulled out of the terminal. By the start of the 1970s, only Amtrak remained in service at the terminal. Amtrak eventually pulled out in 1972, finally leaving the terminal as nothing but an architecturally magnificent shell.

The original plans for the building of the union terminal were much different than the building seen under construction here. The plans originally called for a more classic style, but the company building the terminal brought in two design consultants who changed the entire design to the art deco style shown here. Construction began in 1931 and was completed two years later in 1933. Its purpose was to rid the city of the chaotic system that existed previously. Up until this point, Cincinnati had seven different train stations scattered throughout the city. Catching connecting trains and getting from station to station was a hassle. The union terminal was built to resolve this. The station housed many major railroad companies, including the Cleveland, Cincinnati, Chicago and St. Louis Railway ("the Big Four") and the Baltimore and Ohio Railroad. Today Amtrak has returned to the restored station and still carries 13,000 passengers a year. (Courtesy of the Dan Finfrock collection.)

This photograph depicts work being done to the interior of the union terminal during its construction between 1931 and 1933. The circular structure in the center of the room would eventually become the ticket counter, and the hallway in the center of the picture leads down to the concourse. The wall on the left side of the photograph displays one of the 17 murals to grace the union terminal during its operation. Building designers hired German artist Winold Reiss to create two 110-foot-long and 22-foot-high murals in the rotunda of the building depicting the history of Cincinnati. The mural pictured on the left of this photograph is one of these two murals; the blank wall on the right is where the second mural was eventually placed. These two murals still exist at the same place within the union terminal, while a large mural of a world map and the other 14 murals depicting Cincinnati industry have either been destroyed or moved to the Greater Cincinnati/Northern Kentucky Airport. (Courtesy of the Dan Finfrock collection.)

While the people of Cincinnati realized that the age of train travel had passed, they also wanted something to come of the beautiful Cincinnati Union Terminal. After Amtrak left the station, Southern Railway purchased it in order to run some of its freight trains through the terminal. Since the terminal was built for passenger trains, Southern Railway had to destroy some of the stations so that its taller freight cars would fit. The City of Cincinnati quickly responded by declaring the building a historic landmark. With this status, no one could destroy the building any further.

During the 1980s, the city decided to try to make the terminal into a child-friendly mall and entertainment area with shops, movie theaters, and a bowling alley. Several companies rented space in the terminal to set up this mall, but it did not do well. The shops all soon went out of business.

For almost a decade, the building sat empty and alone.

In 1986, in order to save the building from destruction, the City of Cincinnati decided to try one more time to save the Cincinnati Union Terminal. It voted to turn the terminal into the Cincinnati Museum Center that would one day house the natural history museum and the Cincinnati History Museum.

Since the building had remained empty for so long, massive renovations had to be made in order to make the building suitable for the museums. This occurred most every day in the late 1980s. After night fell, work would stop and the construction workers would go home for the night. Each night a security guard would stay in the building to guard against trespassers. Many pieces of expensive equipment were being used in the renovation, so the security guard had to make sure that all this equipment remained safe throughout the night.

Generally, these nights would be long, quiet, and lonely.

However, that would all change on Wednesday, September 6, 1989. That night was anything but a quiet night. It was a night whose memories still roam these massive hallways at night.

On security detail that night was 50-year-old Shirley A. Baker. She was an 11-month veteran of the terminal security staff, and her night began as every other night. She figured that she would have to endure another long night. Several hours into her shift, things started to go wrong for her. She heard glass break somewhere in the building and went to investigate.

Baker was never seen alive again.

Later on in the night, Baker's manager checked her station to find it empty. For the last 11 months, Baker had never left her station without reporting to him first, so the manager was immediately concerned when he discovered her absence. He tried to find her but eventually alerted the authorities when he realized that something may have happened to her.

The police arrived at the scene around 5:00 a.m. and found several signs that there had been a break-in. There was broken glass, evidence of forced entry, vandalism, and missing radio equipment. Also, the 1986 Oldsmobile that Baker drove was missing from the parking lot. It looked as if the thieves and vandals had kidnapped Baker and escaped in her own car.

Over the next couple of days, her friends and family tried to hold out hope that Baker was okay. The newspapers requested that anyone who knew of her whereabouts contact the police violent crimes division. The papers printed a photograph and reported that she had last been seen in her security uniform on the night of September 6 sometime between 2:30 and 4:30 a.m.

For the next nine weeks, her friends and family searched endlessly for Baker. Then there was a tragic breakthrough in the case; Baker was found in a shallow grave in Clermont County. She had been murdered, but the police still had no explanation for what had happened on the night of September 6.

Through careful police work and trace evidence left by the thieves on the night of the break-in, authorities were finally able to catch three people who were involved in Baker's murder. Two years after the murder, James W. Wetherell, Thomas A. Haynes, and Damon K. Harp were all charged with complicity in the murder.

Through these men, the police were finally able to piece together what had happened that night at the union terminal. Two of the men broke into the terminal around 4:00 or 4:30 a.m. in an attempt to steal some radio equipment to assist them with communication during future burglaries. The third man, James W. Wetherell, was a security guard whose job was to distract Baker as the other two took the radio equipment.

Baker was not so easily distracted, though, and it was not long before she found the two men roaming the halls. As she approached, Haynes, an expert at martial arts, kicked her so that she fell to the floor. He then kicked her several more times until she was dead.

Panicked, the three men carried her out to her car, and they drove away as quickly as they could. They ended up in a remote location in Clermont County where the men had often fished together. Wetherell buried her there.

Even though her body was buried in a shallow grave, some say her spirit never left the Cincinnati Union Terminal. A housekeeper was cleaning the terminal after hours one night and was startled to notice a female security guard that she did not recognize at the end of one of the museum hallways. The housekeeper said hello to the security guard, but the guard did not answer. The housekeeper looked away for a second to clean something and then looked up to see that the guard had vanished. Later the housekeeper asked about the new female security guard and was told that there were not any female security guards on that night. Upon searching the building, no one could find this female security guard that the housekeeper had seen. They figured that it was just the ghost of Baker, watching the place like she had been the night she disappeared.

Housekeepers will often see Baker when cleaning alone at night. Sometimes they will hear footsteps down a hallway around a corner, but when they turn the corner to see who is there, the hallway is empty. Doors will slam down a distant hall without explanation, and housekeepers will often get the feeling that they are being watched, although they are alone.

This has resulted in some of the housekeeping staff refusing to work alone after hours for fear of encountering this ghostly security guard.

The plan by the City of Cincinnati to turn the terminal into the cultural center of the city did finally come to fruition in 1990. Today the building is sectioned off into several different museums and cultural centers. As one walks in the front doors, the Natural History Museum of Cincinnati is to the right. Directly in front, the Omnimax Theater, with its four-story domed Imax screen, sits through a short maze of hallways. A children's museum sits down an escalator to the immediate left. And farther to the left is the entrance to the Cincinnati History Museum. In the lower level, the Cincinnati Historical Society is headquartered. It has an impressive library, which is open to the public.

Shirley A. Baker is not the only ghost who haunts this huge building. Once a man was walking on a tour of the Cincinnati History Museum and happened to glance upward toward the World War II plane that is displayed overhead. He noticed that there was a man sitting in the cockpit of the plane and naturally assumed that the pilot was a mannequin that was supposed to sit in the plane. Later, as he circled back around and glanced back up at the same plane, he noticed that the cockpit was empty. When he asked a museum worker about the pilot in the plane, the worker told him that the plane has always been empty; there had never been a mannequin of a pilot in the cockpit.

Employees at the Cincinnati History Museum have heard people asking about the figure in the plane on more than one occasion. They simply consider it another of the many ghosts that haunt the massive building. Perhaps an old pilot's ghost has returned to the plane to relive some of his most traumatic moments of life.

In 1991, Amtrak returned to the terminal, and it transports passengers around the country to this day. In 2007, more than 13,000 passengers embarked or disembarked their trains from this terminal, a terminal that barely survived through the latter part of the 20th century.

The Cincinnati Union Terminal was a huge depot from 1933 until after World War II. Over 216 trains would pass through this terminal every day. The station saw a countless number of people walk through it, boarding trains and kissing their loved ones goodbye as they left for war. During the Great Depression, the union terminal saw a huge decline in business. Streetcars were being used more often, and people could no longer afford the luxuries of travel. World War II eventually brought passengers back to the station, but after the war ended, many travelers preferred cars or planes to carry them around the country. The union terminal trains stopped carrying passengers altogether by the 1970s. Today, when the platforms are all but empty, people will hear phantom voices. Sometimes these voices sound happy; sometimes it sounds like they are crying. (Courtesy of the Dan Finfrock collection.)

The tracks themselves are said to be haunted. When the tracks are silent, one can hear hustle and bustle although no one is there. Sometimes people hear crying. Perhaps these are echoes of those people who bade farewell to soldiers who left on these tracks but never returned home. People will also sometimes see apparitions of people waving to invisible trains or apparitions of people locked within a joyous embrace. All kinds of emotional echoes seem to live on at these tracks, especially when they are empty and void of life.

The trains do not come as often anymore as they did in their heyday. The wars to which these trains carried soldiers no longer wage on in distant lands. There are planes now, more efficient and rapid than trains could ever hope to be. This may be for the best though.

Memories already fill this place and still echo after all these years.

The Cincinnati Subway: The Unfinished Tracks

If one were to draw a line through the center of the most haunted section of Cincinnati, that line would be Ezzard Charles Drive. On the west end of this road is the Cincinnati Union Terminal, the haunted train station and cultural center where memories of World War II and a murdered security guard haunt its labyrinth. The road dead-ends to the east at Music Hall, arguably the most haunted building in Ohio south of the Ohio State Penitentiary. As if these two ghostly landmarks are not enough to give this short road the title of the most haunted place in Cincinnati, underneath the asphalt, close to the eastern end of the street, lays the defunct Cincinnati Subway.

There are few entrances that remain to these abandoned tunnels, all of which are closed off to the public by impenetrable steel doors. The tunnels on the western side of town were the only ones that were ever built, and some of these have been completely blocked off, without access from the surface or from the other passageways. In fact, only two entrances remain at all, and they are both along Central Parkway, visible along the side of I-75 to those who know where to look.

Inside, the tunnels are dark and forbidding. No electric lights remain. Only glimmers of lights from distant entrances and manhole covers allow anything to be seen at all.

From the underground, it is easy to see the similarity to subways from the bigger cities like New York and Philadelphia. Concrete pillars decorate the stops; long narrow tunnels connect these stations. Graffiti also covers much of the tunnels as vandals had somehow gained entrance to the abandoned maze.

Beyond this, there are a lot of things that seem out of place here. Some of the tunnels are lined with huge water mains that the Cincinnati Water Works installed there after realizing the subway would never come to fruition. One section of the tunnel is lined with wooden benches. Someone had the idea of turning the dark tunnels into a nuclear fallout shelter during the cold war, but that was another idea that was never realized. Perhaps the aspect of these corridors that is most chillingly out of place is the way that all the tunnels eventually lead to a dead end. All the tunnels eventually end in the middle of nowhere, the only escape being to backtrack all the way back to one of the only two entrances. There are seven miles of track that only lead to dead ends.

What happened to this place? Why were the tunnels never finished? Walking through these dark abandoned tunnels almost begs these questions.

Historically, the idea came through a magazine called the *Graphic*. What had happened was that a major canal that ran through the city had become defunct. The upkeep of the canal had become more than the canal itself was worth. The city realized that something had to be done, and it was an article in the *Graphic* that captured the interest of the city. It suggested that instead of filling in the canal with more roads that would add to the congestion in downtown Cincinnati, why not build tunnels and a subway system through the city.

The idea caught on, and suddenly the whole city was caught up in the excitement of having its own subway system. The city council approved a bill giving $6 million toward the creation of

There are not many pieces of the Cincinnati Subway still visible from ground level. Although a few of the tunnels still run underground, there are very few entrances or exits that still exist. This entrance is one of the few and is visible today as one travels southbound down I-75. This entrance rests just below Central Parkway leading into a long dark, dingy tunnel that runs the same direction as Central Parkway does today. Heavy steel gates and steel barriers prevent any unauthorized trespassing into these tunnels. If people were to gain access to the stretches of tunnel that exist, they would see what looks like any station in business today. The stairways that would have led to the ground level still exist, leading up to either a steel gate or leading into nothing. Few scattered benches still sit in the tunnels below. Remains of the construction, pieces of wood and steel, are scattered about.

the city's subway system. Almost as soon as the issue was passed, World War I started in Europe and construction had to be halted. The cost of the building supplies was much too high during the war, and the city felt that it would be better to wait until the war was over and materials like steel and explosives were less expensive.

When the war ended, construction continued. After only completing seven miles of tunnels and not having laid any track, the project ran out of money. Inflation after the war had made the $6 million only a fraction of what was needed to complete the subway system. When the stock market crashed in 1929, the city encountered even more problems in passing legislation that could raise the money for the subway.

By the time the Great Depression ended, World War II had started, and again materials and manpower were far too rare to consider finishing the subway project during the war. Then, after the war, cars had become so popular that the population of Cincinnati was no longer pushing for the completion of the subway.

So the project just kind of died.

The city could not afford to do anything but block the tunnels off and let it deteriorate underground. Many citizens of Cincinnati today do not even know about the dark tunnels that only lead to dead ends. But the lack of escape routes makes the ghosts of these tunnels that much more terrifying.

Legends tell a couple of different stories about the origins of these ghosts. The first story tells of one of the original planners of the subway project hanging himself in one of the tunnels upon learning that his hard work would ultimately go unfinished. Another story tells that several workers died during the construction of the tunnels in their earlier stages of development. These workers are said to haunt the tunnels.

Many ghostly occurrences have been reported here. Many people who walk the tunnels in modern times will hear strange sounds. Footsteps will echo through the tunnels although those inside know that they are the only ones there. Voices will travel through the tunnel despite the fact that no one is speaking. Sounds of work and machinery will carry down the empty passageways. Screams will often be reported echoing distantly in the corridors.

Apparitions have also been encountered here. People will report seeing people working on the tunnels although work ceased long ago. When these workers are approached, they vanish as if they were never there.

Once a group of teenagers decided to break into and explore the supposedly haunted tunnels. Two boys brought their girlfriends into the tunnels, with nothing more than flashlights to illuminate the passageways ahead. After an hour or two of moving deeper and deeper into the tunnels, they noticed something swinging from the ceiling up ahead. They assumed that they were seeing loose wires swinging back and forth since they were fairly certain that they were the only ones in the tunnels. They could not tell what exactly was swinging because their lights were too dim and the swinging shadows were too far away. So the group decided to investigate further.

As the group moved closer and closer to what they had originally assumed was swinging wires, they came to the horrible realization that it was a man with a rope around his neck swinging in the tunnel up ahead.

The girls screamed in terror while the boys cautiously approached the man who appeared to have hung himself. As they approached, he suddenly vanished. Nothing swung in the tunnel up ahead. In fact, nothing obstructed the tunnel, no wires, no hanging vines of any sort. It was just an empty tunnel. The only sound was the crying and panic of the two girls who had seen the apparition.

Had they only encountered a trick of the light, a flashlight silhouetting another member of the group, or had they witnessed the apparition of the man who had reputedly hung himself in

This photograph depicts construction on the Cincinnati Subway at the Miami and Erie Canal bed near Music Hall. The bridge in the background of this photograph was once a bridge whose purpose was to provide pedestrians a way to cross the canal. Eventually the canal could no longer transport goods and passengers as efficiently as roads and railroads, so in 1920, the city decided to build a subway system. The empty canal bed was the perfect place to build much of this new system. It saved the city from having to dig a new path for the subway by allowing it to simply build parts in the basin of the canal and then cover it with dirt and pavement. Today the area depicted in this photograph is Central Parkway; the abandoned subway tunnels still sit underneath the road. (Courtesy of the Cincinnati Museum Center, Cincinnati Historical Society Library.)

the tunnels when he realized that his subway project would never come to fruition? No records exist of such a suicide, but that does not mean it did not happen. Earlier in the century, suicides were often covered up to save the deceased and their family from humiliation and disgrace.

The group of trespassers fled the tunnels that night. Perhaps the whole story is something of an urban myth, just a story passed from person to person, embellished with every successive telling.

The City of Cincinnati itself lost its own dream of having a subway system. In a way these abandoned tunnels echo with the lost dreams of not only those who worked to complete this mass transit system but also everyone in the city who once hoped to ride the underground into the city.

The ghosts cry to this day in disappointment and reminiscence of what might have been.

NETHERLAND PLAZA HOTEL, CINCINNATI

The Carew Tower reaches higher into the sky than any other building along the Cincinnati skyline. The architects at Starrett Brothers Inc. built this and the attached Netherland Plaza Hotel in 1931. The same architects would go on to design the Empire State Building in New York City. The Carew Tower/Netherland Plaza project was huge, and money was tight. The builder, John Emery, became one of the largest employers in the city during the 1930s. The Great Depression had struck Cincinnati, and since Emery had liquidated all his stocks to fund this project, he was one of the only people in town who was hiring. The construction of this massive building required that an average of 1,000 men be working at any given time. The work consisted of laying over four billion bricks, 15,000 tons of steel, and over 30,000 barrels of cement.

Six

DOWNTOWN CINCINNATI

At a glance, downtown may appear sterile. Next to some magnificent historic structures in the outlying areas, the tall skyscrapers of the Cincinnati skyline appear almost uniform and modern. This could not be further from reality. Cincinnati started where these skyscrapers now stand. Many of the most important events in Cincinnati's history occurred inside and around these skyscrapers. Many of the city's most important people lived there among those buildings. Many of the city's most ambitious people died there. Many of those who have died there continue to live on as ghosts, reminding the modern Cincinnatians that they coexist with history.

Omni Netherland Plaza: The Lady in Green

In 1961, the owners of the Omni Netherland Plaza Hotel decided that they would modernize their grand hotel in the heart of downtown Cincinnati. They put down new vinyl floors over the historic floors. They placed new carpeting and covered up a lot of the ornately decorated walls and ceilings with plywood and drywall. The owners felt that this old hotel needed to move its design into modern times.

Thirty years earlier in 1929, the hotel was only an idea. New technology had recently become available to build towers that climbed far above any other structures of the day. The most significant piece of technology that aided in this age of expanding to the sky was the elevator. The height of buildings was no longer limited to how many flights of stairs people were willing to walk.

In 1929, the architectural firm of Shreve, Lamb, and Harmon created the design for the Netherland Plaza Hotel and adjoining Carew Tower in Cincinnati. The designers would later use the same design in order to build the Empire State Building in New York City. Starrett Brothers Inc. was the construction company that was ready to complete the monumental task, which left only the object of money. The builders and designers had to find someone to finance the huge project.

John Emery was the man that they found. He had plenty of assets with which to fund the project, yet the banks in the area all refused to give him a loan. His financial advisors told him that he should back out of the project, but despite their pleas to the contrary, Emery decided to sell all his stocks and securities in order to liquidate his assets and fund the project.

This was actually a huge stroke of luck for him and for the hotel. Just a couple of months after liquidating his stock assets, the stock market crashed in October 1929. He would have lost everything had he not sold the stock. Instead he was able to fund the construction of the Netherland Plaza in the time of the Great Depression when there was not much money to spend. Emery became Cincinnati's single-largest employer during the Great Depression.

In 1930, construction started on the magnificent hotel and adjoining Carew Tower. This magnificent French art deco structure was meant to make life easier for people who lived in the city. There was the hotel, restaurants, a shopping mall, and offices. It was meant to be a city within a city, and it achieved that goal, towering above every other building within the city. At 49 stories tall, 574 feet, the Carew Tower is to this day the tallest structure in Cincinnati.

The 1930s were tough times in Cincinnati, and many people jumped at the opportunity to make money during the Depression by working on the new tower and hotel. It was very dangerous work, and several accidents occurred during the construction of the hotel. The great heights at which the construction took place along with the heavy machinery that was used for the building made the scene an accident waiting to happen.

According to legend, there was one man who fell to his death from the tower in 1930 whose body was never found. The stories go on to say that the man's wife never gave up looking for him. She would go to the construction site wearing her nicest green dress and would absently roam the site wherever she was allowed, looking for any signs of her vanished husband. It is said that even after the building was completed in January 1931, she would still regularly visit the site, searching desperately for her missing husband.

The building was a grand achievement and opened to much critical acclaim in early 1931. The Netherland Plaza Hotel opened with a staggering 800 guest rooms, 11 kitchens, 7 restaurants, a huge ballroom, and the famous Hall of Mirrors, which was modeled after the Hall of Mirrors in the French palace of Versailles. Construction had included at least four billion bricks, 15,000 tons of steel, and 30,000 barrels of cement. It was truly a monumental achievement that brilliantly punctuated the skyline of Cincinnati.

The building opened under the name the St. Netherland Plaza. The *St.* was an abbreviation for the builders' names, the Starretts. The word *Netherland* was used to describe its location. The hotel sat in the area between the Ohio River and the seven hills of northern Cincinnati.

The hotel was the most luxurious in the Cincinnati area, and the era's rich and famous who happened to be passing through the city would stay here. In the late 1930s, Winston Churchill stayed at the hotel. The hotel aptly named the suite in which he stayed the Churchill Suite. Eleanor Roosevelt was also a frequent visitor to the hotel. She stayed at the hotel at least 12 times throughout her lifetime.

In 1942, a disaster occurred at the tower. For some unknown reason, a fire broke out on the fifth floor of the hotel. Luckily, there were sprinkler systems in place that were able to control and eventually extinguish the fire. Unfortunately, though, the water from the sprinklers caused great amounts of damage to the Hall of Mirrors and other rooms on the fifth floor of the building. No one was killed in the blaze, but the building itself would suffer irreversible damage from the incident.

A greater tragedy occurred at the Netherland Plaza on May 31, 1956. A 25-year-old woman named Norma Jean Haller had recently been released from a mental sanatorium. Three weeks earlier she had attempted to kill herself by throwing herself in front of a moving bus. The bus's driver was able to react in time, and passersby were able to rescue her from the street. When she was admitted to the mental asylum, it was discovered that she was five months pregnant.

At home in Springdale, she had a husband and two children who were anxiously awaiting her release from the asylum and return to a life of normality. It was something that would never happen.

Although those at the sanatorium felt that she was ready for release, she was still determined to end her life. She went to downtown Cincinnati in order to find a tall enough building to jump from. She found the site of her suicide when she looked up at the towering Netherland Plaza Hotel.

Instead of taking the elevator, she climbed the stairs to the 28th floor of the building, and she wrote a note. She wrote the note on a napkin that she had picked up in the lobby. It said, "My name is Jean Haller, call my husband. Children will be better off." She gently placed the note in the stairwell and climbed out of a window onto a small ledge between the 28th and 29th floors of the hotel.

While on the ledge, she wrote another note and placed it on the ledge from which she planned to jump. It read, "Please call my husband and tell him I'm sorry."

Then she jumped. It was 6:55 p.m.

An office worker who worked on the 16th floor of the Carew Tower heard a scream come from outside his window. Then he heard a dull thud. He looked out of his window and saw blood streaked across the wall and Haller's body lying across the areaway near the hotel.

Her body lay on the roof between the Carew Tower and Netherland Plaza Hotel. She did not appear dead. She simply appeared asleep. Her hand was against her flowered shirt. Her slippers were on the roof several feet away.

John Haller, her husband, was called to the General Hospital. It was not until he entered the lobby that they informed him that his wife had killed herself. They asked if he would identify the body. He looked dazed and refused to go look at the body. He told the hospital staff that his children were at home with his brother Neil and he should go back to take care of them.

To this day people will sometimes hear screams and sobbing coming from the stairwell between the 28th and 29th floors.

These are not the only fatalities to occur at this hotel. Beyond those killed during construction and the woman who committed suicide in 1956, at least one man died suddenly of a heart attack when entering the lobby of the hotel. A 52-year-old manager of the Safety Equipment Manufacturers Association in New York named Richard Armstrong was registered at the hotel for a three-day stay. He was in town for business purposes, and as he entered the lobby, he collapsed. He was dead by the time the medics arrived on the scene.

Employees will hear footsteps in the lobby, even when there is no one there. Perhaps these footsteps are remnants of this businessman from New York who died so unexpectedly there.

Over the next few years even more famous people would spend time in the Netherland Plaza Hotel. Elvis Presley would always stay at the hotel when he would tour anywhere nearby. John and Jackie Kennedy visited the hotel on occasion as well. The Kennedys once attended a political gala that occurred in the Hall of Mirrors in 1959.

But the hotel would begin to lose its historic art deco charm when the renovations began in 1961. All the great art deco design and sculpture from around the building was covered up to make way for modernization. The hotel took on an entirely different look and lost its 1920s charm, which it had held throughout the first 30 years of its existence.

In 1981, though, the owners of the hotel realized that the true beauty and power of this giant hotel was not in the modernization that had been overtaking it since the 1960s but in its original art deco decor. The owners decided that they would restore the great hotel to its original beauty and would tear up all the linoleum and carpeting that were placed to hide its historical brilliance.

Despite the risk of losing money, the owners shut down the entire hotel for a period of two years to restore it. Work went by smoothly and on schedule until it neared completion in 1983. In 1983, strange things began to happen, which helped to give the hotel its reputation as one of the most haunted hotels in America.

A construction worker who arrived early to the site walked into the Hall of Mirrors to begin to plan the day's restoration work. When he entered the room, a woman wearing a green dress was standing on the other side of the room. She appeared to be looking around at all the equipment that was lying on the floor. The construction worker knew that no one was supposed to be in the room at all so he called out to her, asking her who she was and what she was doing here. She looked back nervously and walked into a doorway at the back of the room.

The construction worker assumed at this point that the woman was trespassing since she ran away when she saw him, so he followed her into the door at the back. He looked around and did not see her anywhere. He saw no place where she could have gone.

A couple of days later, men were working on the mezzanine level of the hotel when they saw a similar woman dressed in green appear and start watching them while they did their work. The group of them assumed that she worked with the hotel but thought that her green dress seemed outdated. She did not say anything as she stood there, and eventually she simply vanished.

The Hall of Mirrors shown in this photograph is a gorgeous room used as a venue for weddings, dinners, and other events. This room was built as a reconstruction of the Hall of Mirrors in the palace at Versailles near Paris, France. Since its construction, the room has changed several times. This large ornate room is said to be the home of the lady in green. Supposedly, this ghost is that of a young woman who is forever searching the hotel for her missing husband. Legends say that her husband was killed and his body lost during construction of the Netherland Plaza Hotel. She still roams the halls in a green dress, looking for her lost love.

Most of the building in which the Taft Theater is housed was built as a Masonic temple. The Masonic temple still exists today, but the section of the building on the corner of Fifth and Main Streets was designated as a theater in the early 1930s. Much of the theater was decorated in art deco style, which gave it a very modern appearance next to many of the other buildings in downtown in the 1930s. Pictured here, the front doors of the theater lead into the box office and auditorium. The overhang has recently been renovated to appear more like it did when the theater opened in the 1930s. The poster cases that flank the door are from the 1930s and still read "Taft Auditorium" across the top.

The workers admitted that they did not see her vanish. They were concentrating on their work, only glancing up at the strange visitor from time to time. One time they glanced up and she simply was not there. They assumed that she had just sneaked away while they were not looking, but then rumors started flying around the job site about this mysterious lady in green.

Several more times during the restoration work in 1983, workers saw the lady in green. She would watch the work being done with interest and then suddenly run away or simply vanish. Soon everyone at the job site had either seen or heard about this lady in green who was stalking the workers while they worked. The only places that she was ever seen were on the mezzanine level, the Hall of Mirrors, and the small chapel that sat near the Hall of Mirrors.

To this day, employees at the Omni Netherland Plaza report seeing the lady in green from time to time. This happens so often in fact that a blurb in the brochure talks about the lady in green. It says that the woman in green is the ghost of the woman whose husband disappeared during construction. It says that she still searches the hotel for his body to this day.

People know the Omni Netherland Plaza as a world-class hotel, perhaps the most luxurious and historic in all of Cincinnati. It has become a member of the Historic Hotels of America group. This is a group of over 200 hotels across the country that share great historical significance with one another. Famous people of the modern day also choose to stay in the Netherland Plaza Hotel when they stay the night in Cincinnati. Celine Dion and Jodie Foster have spent the night here. George H. W. Bush, former president of the United States, has also stayed here at the haunted hotel.

And yet, despite all these years that have passed, despite all the hotel's awards and famous patrons, despite everything that has happened to it throughout its history, memories of the darkest tragedies of the building's history remain. Screams and footsteps still echo through these historic halls, and a woman in a green dress still roams here looking for her lost husband who mysteriously disappeared during construction.

Taft Theater: Cigar Smoke

The stage at the Taft Theater is still in use today. The hustle and bustle of preparing for performances still imbues the theater with a sense of life. The theater lives on in all its glory even to this day. The seats on the floor and those above on the balcony level are still filled week after week, month after month; people are still anxious to walk through the doors and experience the performances.

The Taft Theater was built in the early 1930s, and it utilized the art deco architectural and design style that was so prevalent in the city during that time frame. Structures such as the Cincinnati Union Terminal and Netherland Plaza Hotel were built in the same time period and share a common architectural and design scheme with the Taft Theater. The theater consists of 2,500 seats, all of which have an unobstructed view of the stage.

The ghost stories that circulate about this place tend to be vague and are confined to only the darkest and most remote corners of the upper balcony. The primary ghost of this theater takes on a unique form; instead of an apparition, disembodied sounds, or phantom chills, this ghost takes the form of a smell.

It is said that sometimes in the dark corners of the upper balcony at the Taft Theater, one can smell cigar smoke lingering in the air. This smell of smoke has no discernible source; in fact it has been illegal to smoke inside the building for many years.

Once, after a show had ended and all the patrons had finished filing out of the building, an usher was in the auditorium sweeping up. As he was sweeping the bottom level of the theater, he suddenly got the feeling that he was being watched. This feeling struck him so hard and so suddenly that he stopped what he was doing and looked around for anyone.

As he looked around the building, his eyes focused on a figure that was standing in the corner up on the second balcony of the theater. The usher was surprised by what the man was wearing. He was wearing a top hat and 19th-century clothing. The man on the balcony was smoking a cigar as he looked down on the usher.

Confused, the usher decided that he would head up to the balcony and find out about this man. The show that had just finished did not use costumes from the 1800s, so the usher saw no reason that a man dressed in that way should be in the building. When the usher climbed the stairs and emerged on the second balcony of the theater, there was no one there. When the usher went over to the corner where he had seen the figure, he did sense some evidence that he had not imagined the whole thing. He could smell the cigar smoke from the cigar he had seen the man smoking.

Reports of this shadowy man in the top hat on the second balcony are not as common as those of just the cigar smells, but there have been several instances where people have seen this man. Their descriptions of him are all hauntingly similar.

Perhaps this man was someone who frequented the theater in life and decided to continue his patronage through death. Perhaps this man experienced some traumatic event in this building or chose to come back because this was where he experienced his happiest moments. The apparition never speaks or acts, only smokes his cigars and vanishes when someone approaches.

Perhaps the apparition is only a trick of the light and the cigar smoke is just a fault with the ventilation system or smells from long ago baked permanently into some aged fabrics. Are the witnesses to these phenomena simply creating these ghosts from unlikely shadows, or can an atmosphere of a place exist supernaturally through smells and shadows in the darkest corners?

Taft Museum: Anna and the Lady in Pink

Time completely forgot about the Taft house. As the skyscrapers and asphalt jungle of downtown Cincinnati grew by the Ohio River, the Taft house remained untouched. Towering above, the city stands sentinel, unnoticing of the two-story 19th-century home that sits alone, far below.

Turning down Pike Street on the eastern edge of downtown, one is immediately taken by the sight of the house. The dull gray and brown of the city is sharply contrasted by the lawn and walk leading up to this house. One does not realize how colorless the downtown atmosphere is until the vibrant red, yellow, and green of the lawn and flower-lined walk contrast sharply with its colorlessness.

The house itself stands impressively despite those larger buildings that surround it. Its architecture is quite beautiful, with balconies, columns, and large windows decorating its two stories. The double door at the front looms menacingly taller than anyone who climbs those few stairs to the front porch. It is considered the greatest example of the Federal style of architecture in Cincinnati. The original front door to the building is no longer the entrance though.

Currently, the entrance to the house and museum is around the back in a modern extension that was built there during renovations to house the special art exhibits that from time to time will come to the museum. The modern entrance consists of two glass doors leading to a short staircase and the front desk of the museum. Behind the desk sits the entrance of the museum and the gift shop. To the right of the desk sits the backyard and a view of the back of the house.

In 1812, a man named Martin Baum purchased this land just outside the city limits and decided to build the house there. The house was completed in 1820.

Martin Baum himself was a major figure in the history of Cincinnati. He was the son of German immigrants and moved to Cincinnati from Maryland in 1794. He owned several businesses in the city, including a sugar refinery and a foundry. He also built steamboats and owned real estate across the city. He brought in many German immigrants to work at his businesses and is largely responsible for the high German population in Cincinnati today.

It was due to these businesses and the success that they experienced that Baum became the city's first millionaire. He used his wealth and power to get himself elected mayor in 1807. He was the city's third mayor. He excelled at his job and is considered one of the city's greatest leaders in its history.

As soon as he finished building the house in 1820, he and his businesses were caught in a financial upheaval, and by 1825, he was forced to deed his house back to the Bank of the United States. Baum would live six more years before dying in an influenza outbreak in 1831.

The house was then bought by David Sinton, who moved into the house with his daughter Anna. David Sinton became a very wealthy man because of a scheme he arrived at where he would stockpile as much iron as he could until the Civil War broke out and then he would sell that iron at inflated cost. His plan worked beautifully, and he quickly became the richest man in the state of Ohio.

His daughter Anna, David's only surviving child, would inherit the house from him and marry into the Taft family, the most powerful family in Cincinnati at the time. She married Charles Phelps Taft, the half brother of the future president of the United States, William Howard Taft.

Anna and Charles would live happily together in the house for many years, from 1873 until 1927. Charles ran a media empire, owning a newspaper and other media outlets during this time, but he always had time for this beautiful house so near his beloved Cincinnati. The house was so impressive that William Howard Taft actually accepted his presidential nomination from the front room of the building in 1908.

Anna and Charles were avid art lovers, and they accrued a collection of art over their years in the house. Eventually Anna and Charles moved away from the house and donated the house itself and the art inside for the benefit of the people of Cincinnati. Since then, it has become a museum and still looks much as it did when the family lived there almost a century ago.

Over the years, though, the house had become very important to those who lived there. It was both a status symbol and a major part of their lives, where they would relax and spend the most important years of their lives. It is no wonder that every now and again a ghost story will emerge about this old building seemingly out of place in the middle of downtown.

The gift shop is haunted. The gift shop is just a little room lined by shelves with a cashier's counter in the back left corner. Since the gift shop has existed, ghost stories have circulated from employee to employee.

Once an employee was closing up the gift shop for the night. Besides closing up the register, the employee checked closely to make sure that everything was in order on the shelves. Satisfied, she left for the night. The house remained abandoned all throughout the evening hours until opening time the next morning. When the opener came into the shop the next morning, though, a handful of items from the shelves were laid strewn across the floor. It seemed as if someone had come in during the night and pushed the items off the shelves and across the floor—perhaps a ghost who did not want the gift shop in its house.

This story seems to happen again and again. A cashier will close up the shop for the night, making sure everything is in order, and the cashier who comes in the next morning will see the merchandise strewn across the floor.

Another ghostly occurrence happened when there was a group eating a celebration dinner in the back courtyard of the house. Everyone was eating and occupied with their own conversations, but one of the partygoers looked up to the second-floor balcony of the house. Up on the balcony he saw a woman dressed in 19th-century clothing looking down into the courtyard at the partygoers. The man who saw her did not mention it to anyone else. He assumed that an employee from the house was dressed up for some other event and she had wandered out onto the balcony to view the festivities. Later on that night, he asked an employee about her and asked why she was dressed like that.

Along Pike Street, just east of downtown Cincinnati, this two-story, 19th-century home welcomes visitors. The greenery stands out in the midst of the otherwise gray buildings that surround it. A man by the name of Martin Baum built this house in 1820 after purchasing the land eight years prior. Soon after the completion of the house, Baum ran into financial troubles and lost the house. David Sinton gained ownership of the house and moved in with his daughter Anna. After David's death, Anna inherited the home. In 1873, Anna married Charles Phelps Taft, the half brother of William Howard Taft. Anna and Charles lived in the house until 1927 when they donated all the art they had collected and the house itself to the city of Cincinnati. Today the home is the Taft Museum of Art, which displays the beautiful works Anna and Charles had collected.

Behind the house, this large courtyard and balcony are commonly used for large events, such as parties and weddings. The landscaping and ornate decor make this the perfect setting for any elegant party. During parties, however, uninvited guests will sometimes arrive. The most commonly reported of these ghostly party guests is that of a young lady who appears on the second-floor balcony. This lady is always dressed in clothing that appears to be from the 19th century. She simply watches the event and never speaks with anyone. Eventually she walks into the house and vanishes from sight. Many claim that this lady is the ghost of Anna Taft.

The employee assured him that there were no employees dressed in that manner and that there were no employees in that section of the house. In fact, there was no access to the second-floor balcony looking over the courtyard, so it could not have even been a patron.

The employee had heard stories about this same ghost. Apparently this had not been the first time that someone had seen an apparition similar to this. The employee described in detail what the woman looked like. The man was amazed and confirmed that that was exactly what he had seen. The employee said that it was the ghost of Anna Taft. A lot of times, Anna is seen walking out on the balcony, especially when there is some event going on in the courtyard.

In the museum there was a picture of what Anna looked like in life. When the employee showed the man the picture, he turned white. He was sure she was the same woman that he had seen on the balcony.

A third ghost story about this house is the story of the lady in pink. The museum consists of a main hallway with several rooms off to either side of it. The only access into and out of these rooms is through that main hallway. Security guards and patrons alike will often report seeing a lady in a pink 19th-century dress walking down the hall and vanishing into one of the rooms. If anyone is to follow this lady in pink into one of these rooms, he or she will find that room empty, as if the lady in pink had never been there.

The lady in pink has attained an ominous reputation in the house. Once a security guard was walking the main hallway. There were no patrons in the museum at the time, so the guard was simply walking the halls to make sure that everything was in order. Suddenly chills crept down his spine, and he got the feeling that he was being watched. He looked around but saw no one else in the house. As he turned back toward the end of the hallway, he heard a female voice whispering in his ear. He could not describe exactly what was being said, only that the whispers were threatening.

The guard spun around toward the front door, expecting the whisperer to be behind him, but there was no one there. He slowly turned back toward the end of the hallway and saw the lady in pink glaring at him. He froze, and the lady in pink walked into one of the rooms.

Cautiously the guard began to walk toward the room that he had seen her walk into. He had heard the stories around the house and was convinced that he had just witnessed the menacing lady in pink. He had to be sure, though, so he began walking toward the room at the far end of the hall.

As he neared the doorway, the door suddenly slammed shut. He tried to open the door but was unable. He could easily turn the handle, but the door would not budge. It was as if someone was holding it from the other side.

The guard had finally had enough of tackling this phenomenon by himself, so he went to enlist the help of other employees in the house. He knew that he was risking ridicule if he told them that he had seen a ghost, so he simply said that a door had slammed shut and for some reason or another it would not open. Several employees returned to the door, and they all attempted to open it together. It was still stuck.

It took a lot of force, but the group was finally able to get the door open far enough to see what was preventing them from opening it. A chair had been lodged behind the door, underneath the door handle. There were no other entrances to the room. The employees knew that whoever had placed the chair in front of the door was still somewhere in the room.

When they were finally able to get the door open far enough to enter, they were shocked to realize that there was no one in the room. Somehow the chair had moved by itself and lodged itself underneath the door. An intruder could not even have exited through a window. The windows had not been opened in years and they were painted shut.

It was at this point that the security guard finally felt comfortable telling everyone about his ghostly encounter with the lady in pink. The other employees then told the security guard about their own encounters. In almost all cases, they would be filled with a sense of dread, as if something evil was watching them, then they would see the lady in pink walk across the hallway and then vanish into one of the rooms.

Could this lady in pink be the ghost of Anna, upset over having intruders in her house, or is she the ghost of another person from the house's rich history? Perhaps it is the ghost of Martin Baum's wife, upset over the house being taken away from them by the government. Perhaps she is the ghost of Anna's mother and David Sinton's wife, Jane Ellison Sinton, upset that her daughter had given away the beautiful house to be turned into a museum. Whatever the case may be, this lady in pink seems to be angry with those who see her.

Walking through the house, it is easy to see how ghost stories could develop about it. The interior of the house is dark and abnormally silent. The exterior of the house feels like a different world from the gray world of skyscrapers just beyond.

It almost feels as if time forgot to remind this place that it was moving on. The house is the same as it was almost 200 years ago. Perhaps the Taft house's ghostly residents have also become immune to the passage of time. Perhaps they are unwilling to coexist with the present.

Seven

NORTHEAST CINCINNATI

Knights from the Middle Ages were created in order to have a class whose main objective was to preserve values such as faith, loyalty, courage, and honor. Throughout history these values have remained the same, but the definition of faith, loyalty, and honor always vary according to the knight's allegiance and the time at which the knight lived.

Courage, though, is definite. It is clearly defined and does not change according to creed or country. Courage is the will needed to stand strong against one's biggest fear. How many of these knights feared death? Did those who faced death without fear conquer it?

Loveland Castle: Knights of the Golden Trail

The story of Loveland Castle or Chateau La Roche, as it was dubbed by its creator, is one of the strangest yet most inspiring stories to come out of southwestern Ohio. The story starts near the outbreak of World War I when Harry Andrews was a soldier stationed at Fort Dix in New Jersey.

Soon after Harry Andrews arrived at the camp, Fort Dix was hit by a terrible plague where 7,000 soldiers were struck with the deadly disease cerebrospinal meningitis. Andrews was one of the soldiers who fell victim to this terrible disease. He was soon labeled as deceased and was moved to the morgue.

Since the disease was so widespread in the fort, it was quite some time before the doctors were able to attend to Andrews's body. Eventually, though, they were able to move him onto the dissection table where they could do further tests in order to more fully understand this disease that was running rampant through the base.

Before they cut him open, they scraped skin off the inside of his mouth for further testing, then decided to test out a new method for restarting one's heart that had recently come into favor. They put adrenaline into a syringe and inserted the adrenaline directly into Andrews's heart. To their absolute shock, his heart began to beat again.

Still the doctors did not hold out any hope that Andrews would survive the ordeal. He still could not see and was completely paralyzed throughout his entire body. But again, to their surprise, Andrews started to get better. He was unable to eat very much during the first few weeks following the adrenaline shot, and his weight dropped below 90 pounds. But Andrews was unwilling to give up and was soon able to eat more and begin gaining the weight that he needed in order to survive. His sight and full motion did eventually return, and he was able to fully recover from the terrible disease.

Of the original 7,000 men who were infected with the disease at Fort Dix, Andrews was one of only two who survived. Andrews was instrumental in preventing future outbreaks from becoming as deadly though. Antibodies from his blood were used to prevent the further spread of the disease.

Since Harry Andrews had completely recovered, he was sent to France to fight in World War I. He was stationed at Chateau La Roche, an old renaissance castle that had been converted into an army hospital during the war. In World War I, during an especially bloody battle in a field near the Chateau La Roche, Andrews heroically rushed onto the battlefield and pulled a

This castle is known as Chateau La Roche or Loveland Castle and stands today as a historic site in Loveland. A single man named Harry Andrews dedicated his life to building this magnificent structure with his bare hands. In the beginning, he found the stones along the shore of the Little Miami River. When he ran short of stones from the river, he continued by making his own by pouring concrete into milk cartons. His inspiration for the castle was his fascination with the European castles he saw while overseas in World War I. When he returned to the United States, he became the leader of a Boy Scout troop he called the Knights of the Golden Trail. Andrews felt that these knights deserved their own castle. Today the men of the Knights of the Golden Trail own and operate this incredible historic castle in southwest Ohio. (Courtesy of the Knights of the Golden Trail.)

wounded soldier to safety. The story goes on to say that the man he pulled off the battlefield was the son of an English nobleman, and as a reward for saving his son and for his bravery in the face of enemy fire, the English nobleman knighted Andrews.

Before the war, Andrews had been engaged to his high school sweetheart, whom he loved very much. When he returned home after the war, though, he found that she had married someone else. Apparently what had happened was the army never fixed the glitch in the paperwork that said that Andrews had died from the cerebrospinal meningitis. Officials from the army had visited his fiancée and had told her the bad news—that Andrews had died of the disease.

Crushed by the loss of his love, Andrews went on to better himself in whatever ways he could. He studied architecture at Colgate University and Toulouse University and earned a degree in architecture. He also decided that he would help his community by leading a Boy Scout troop.

In 1927, the *Cincinnati Enquirer* was holding a promotion where it would give small tracts of land near the Little Miami River away to anyone who purchased an entire year's subscription to the newspaper. Andrews encouraged his Boy Scout troop to purchase the year's subscription. They did, and the troop was able to use the land that it had attained as a campground.

Every camping season, the Boy Scouts would set up their tents on their land on the banks of the Little Miami River and would camp there. This was always their favorite time of the year and was the experience in the Boy Scouts that they all remembered best. Unfortunately, though, the camp would often be torn up by the elements when they would return the following season. Andrews decided that the best way to remedy this problem would be to build small tents out of stone.

He had the Boy Scouts grab stones from the river, and with the stones, they were able to engineer two small rooms that could be used in their campground. These stone rooms gave Andrews an idea. From his experiences in Europe and from his knowledge of history, he had a great respect for the knights who had been instrumental in bringing Europe out of the Dark Ages. He decided that he would shape his Boy Scouts after the ideals of the European knights. He named his Boy Scout troop the Knights of the Golden Trail.

Then he decided that his knights needed a castle. So he built one with his bare hands.

In 1929, Andrews began building his castle. Since he had a degree in architecture and he had seen castles throughout his time in Europe, he had a very clear idea of what needed to be done in order to build his castle. When he was unable to find enough stones in the river that were of the proper size, he decided to make his own stones. He took milk cartons and filled them with concrete. These concrete blocks were all of the proper size and were simple to duplicate. Most of the castle was built using these milk carton stones.

Since Harry Andrews was slighted by his fiancée, he never fell in love again. He grew older without any family, so he was able to spend most all of his time building his castle. By 1955, he had completed enough of the castle that he could move in and actually live there. People from around the city were amazed by the creation. It was an impressive castle, made even more impressive by the fact that one man had built it all alone.

At least 50 women from the area proposed marriage to Andrews, wanting to live in a real castle right here in Loveland. Andrews turned them all down though. At one point, Andrews tried to collect his army pension. They gave him a very difficult time, though, since according to their records, he was dead. In his later years, Andrews had to get by on social security.

Andrews did complete the castle and lived out the rest of his years there. On March 14, 1981, Andrews was burning trash just outside the castle doors. As the fire began to simmer out, he stomped on the ashes to put the fire completely out. As he stomped on the fire, the leg of his pants caught fire. As he struggled to put out his burning pants, the rest of his pants caught fire.

He called for help, and some people nearby rushed to his aid. They were too late though; his legs were burned quite badly. The doctors attempted skin grafts to save him, but he was too old

This photograph shows Sir Harry Andrews working in his bedroom office. Today the room looks much the same with the desk and typewriter sitting in the same position. Andrews was born in 1890, joined the army in 1914, and was sent to France soon thereafter. From there, he successfully saved an English nobleman's son from dying on the battlefield near Chateau La Roche and was knighted by this nobleman. Soon after his return to the United States in 1927, Andrews acquired a small plot of land from a special promotion the Cincinnati Enquirer offered, and he began building this castle in 1929. Twenty-six years later, in 1955, Andrews completed enough of the castle to move in and make it his permanent residence. Over the next 26 years, he completed the castle. He died in a freak accident at the castle in March 1981. (Courtesy of the Knights of the Golden Trail.)

This photograph shows that the beauty of Andrews's craftsmanship extended beyond the exterior of the castle. This chapel sits on the second level. This room has seen a great deal of paranormal activity. Sir Fred told about a particular occurrence captured by a local northern Kentucky paranormal investigation team. According to Sir Fred, the team had a camera facing the door of the chapel throughout the investigation. The door has the light switch in the upper left corner. The switch is a dimmer switch that must be rotated in order to gain full brightness. Even though the room was dark in the video and with the infrared camera it was clear that no one entered or exited the room, the lights suddenly flipped to full brightness in the video. The paranormal investigators were unable to come up with any explanation for this. (Courtesy of the Knights of the Golden Trail.)

for the procedures to work properly. He died from his injuries from the fire just a couple of weeks later. He deeded the castle to the Knights of the Golden Trail.

The Knights of the Golden Trail continue to run the castle to this day. But they will often report other strange forces and figures that inhabit these stone rooms and hallways.

The first ghost stories to come out of the castle actually came from Andrews himself. He would report that strange things would often happen in the castle at all hours of the day. He said that oftentimes visitors would be in the castle and when they were misbehaving in any way, shape, or form, they would get a slight electric shock. Andrews said that it was the ghost who took up residence in the castle, keeping all the visitors in line.

But beyond this, Andrews himself did experience a variety of things in the castle that he had trouble explaining away. He said that these happenings would always occur past midnight, when the castle had been dark and he had been the only one in the castle. He said that he would hear footsteps roaming the hallways from time to time and see shadows that had no reason for being there.

The most annoying habit of his ghost, though, was something else entirely. Many times in the middle of the night, he would hear someone knocking loudly at the front door or someone would ring the doorbell. When he went down to check who was knocking at his door at such an unusual time, there was never anyone at the door.

As this went on night after sleepless night, Andrews began to assume that the person knocking at the door was a teenager from town causing trouble. He came up with a system where anyone for whom he cared to answer the door would knock with a secret knock so that he could tell the difference between the pranksters and the people for whom he should answer.

Once he heard the knock in the middle of the night and again assumed that it was the pranksters. It had just recently snowed, so there was a fresh layer of snow that completely covered all the castle grounds. Andrews figured that this was his chance to find out once and for all whether the knocking was in fact teenage pranksters from town. He went to the door and opened it, expecting to see footprints in the fresh snow. There was nothing there. No one had disturbed the snow up to the door since the snow had fallen earlier in the evening.

Andrews reported another ghost that haunted the castle grounds. He said that from the roof of the castle people could see a figure in a willow tree that sat adjacent to the building. The figure was shaped like an egg and had two glowing eyes that would look up at the visitors on the roof. Sometimes the figure would start to move toward the castle, and the visitors would become frightened. Sometimes the women would actually faint when it began to move toward them.

Throughout the years after Andrews's death, people have continued to see ghosts on the castle grounds. Once a volunteer at the castle was doing maintenance on the building with another volunteer. As they were working, they heard the door to the bathroom off the ballroom slam shut. They figured that a trespasser had snuck into the castle, so they rushed up to the ballroom to see who was there. After an exhaustive search, they could not find anyone in the castle.

This happened again to the same two workers. They were in another section of the castle when suddenly the same bathroom door slammed shut again. They rushed to see who was there and found the building empty. One of the workers then figured that the ghost who was slamming the door was trying to tell them something. He figured that the ghost was saying that there was something wrong with the bathroom. He checked the bathroom exhaustively, making sure that everything was in working order. It was, and he even went outside to check the pipes that led into the bathroom. To his surprise, he found that the septic tank was about to overflow. They were able to fix the problem before it became any worse. The slamming door had averted disaster.

Another ghost that still haunts the castle grounds can be traced back to an accident that occurred near the castle during the days when Andrews still lived there. Down by the river, a couple had a moonshine operation in a small cave. One day disaster struck. There was a large

The 20th Century Theater, built in August 1941, sits in Oakley on Madison Road. The theater stands alongside many other buildings, but its old-fashioned marquee towers above everything else, making it stand out. The theater is a leftover of the neighborhood movie theaters that all went out of business in the early 1980s. While many neighborhood theaters were torn down to make way for the multiplex, the 20th Century survived by becoming a venue for large events like concerts and weddings. Just inside the front door there is a large lobby. A kitchen and staircase are on the left. Up the stairs there is a VIP room with a bar and pool table for guests to enjoy before their event. Through the VIP room, another door leads one to the balcony and the projection booth. Straight ahead is this auditorium. This room has space for over 250 guests on the lower level and another 100 or more people on the balcony.

explosion that rocked the small cave, and Andrews and several of the Knights of the Golden Trail rushed down to the river to see what had happened.

They saw smoke billowing out of the small cave, and when the smoke cleared and it became safe to enter the cave, they walked in to find out what had happened. Inside the cave, they found the body of a woman underneath a whiskey barrel. She had been killed in the blast.

Many times since then, visitors and employees at the Loveland Castle have seen an apparition of a woman who they always trace back to the incident at the river.

Once a woman was doing a perimeter check of the castle when she noticed a female figure standing down by the main road. The figure was whitish in color, and as it started to move closer to her, she realized that the figure was transparent. She described the figure as having shoulder-length hair and a long billowy dress. The worker stood there frightened as the ghostly figure moved closer and closer to her. As the figure reached the garden, though, it mysteriously vanished into thin air.

Visitors and other workers have also seen this same woman in white roaming around the castle grounds. They always describe her the same way, and she always vanishes mysteriously right before their eyes.

Another ghost roams the castle, which could be the spirit of Andrews himself. Once a couple was spending the night alone in the castle. As Ron, a worker at the castle, was in the shower, the other worker, Christie, was waiting in the ballroom. As she waited in the ballroom she looked over to the spiral staircase that led up to Andrews's original bedroom and saw a shadow slowly climbing the stairs. The light from down the stairs showed the shadowy silhouette growing larger and larger as it got nearer to the place where she would be able to see it.

She panicked and decided to run away. She fled to the bathroom where Ron was showering and started to bang on the door. She saw that the silhouette was following her down the hallway. The same shadow slowly advanced just beyond where she could see it. When Ron finally opened the door to see what the matter was, the lurking shadow vanished. They decided to spend the night elsewhere and leave the castle for the night.

The castle by itself is a remarkable and unique achievement. One man created a working castle on an unassuming riverbank in Loveland. He spent most of his life completely focused on his castle and on the ideals he set out for his original Boy Scout troop, the Knights of the Golden Trail.

But even after the man who created this wondrous place died, the building has been host to a series of strange phenomena. Have ghosts from the area decided to simply take up residence in the spooky castle by the river, or has Andrews chosen to spend his afterlife in the place where he spent so many of his living years?

Oakley: Film Noir

In 1941, Fox Studios released a movie called *Blood and Sand*. The film is about a bullfighter whose greatest ambition is to become the greatest bullfighter in the world. He gains huge success, runs into personal problems, and eventually is shamed and back to where he started. While everything in his life seems to be going poorly, he knows that he is the best at what he does. He knows that he is a great bullfighter, and he would stop at nothing to prove this to the world. He decides to have one more bullfight to prove to everyone that he is great at his job.

He gets gored by the bull.

This is a lot like many ghost stories. Someone dies unable to continue doing whatever it is that they love, so they come back to continue to complete their ambition. Unfortunately, these ghosts seem to repeat themselves like a broken record. If the hero in the film came back as a ghost, he would be forced to die painfully again and again throughout eternity.

In 1941, plans were finalized to build a movie theater in the town of Oakley, just northeast of Cincinnati. It was going to be a magnificent theater that would draw people from all over the city. It was the very first air-conditioned theater in Cincinnati. It was also one of the first fireproof buildings that was built in the Cincinnati area, and it was slated to be the first place in Cincinnati that offered free valet parking.

The theater was called the 20th Century Theater, and it opened in August 1941. On opening night, the theater showed the film *Blood and Sand* starring Tyrone Power and Rita Hayworth. The theater originally met with huge success as the people living in the area were in desperate need of a neighborhood theater in which to watch the new movies as they were released.

Throughout most of the middle 1900s, this theater continued to be a popular entertainment spot within Cincinnati. All the most popular films of the time would come to this theater, and the people who would come to see the films would remember them as some of their fondest memories.

This would all change in the 1970s. Multiplex theaters were coming into existence around this time. People would flock to the multiplex theaters, leaving the single-screen neighborhood movie houses to decay. The 20th Century Theater turned to running second-run movies for a while during the 1970s. Eventually, though, it was forced to close down in 1983. It was just one in the long list of Cincinnati neighborhood theaters to fall victim to the multiplex.

For the next seven years, the theater would remain abandoned. Vandals would sometimes break into the building and deface it. Water would leak into the building and cause further damage. The building would soon degrade into horribly unsafe and unsanitary conditions. Many citizens of Oakley began fighting to have the old theater torn down.

There was an ongoing argument in Oakley between those who wanted to tear down the old blighted theater and those who wanted to save the historic landmark. The ones who wanted to save the building ended up winning the fight, and in 1990, a man named Mike Belmont purchased the 20th Century Theater and began the extensive renovations that were needed.

When Belmont bought the theater, he did so with the intention of using the building for retail. The building was in a good spot for retail, and the imposing storefront of the defunct theater would help to bring in more customers. Once renovations were finally finished in 1991, the building became Belmont's Floor Company.

The new location for his flooring store at the 20th Century Theater did not go as well as he had hoped, so he pulled his store out of the building and to a different location in Oakley in 1992. Later that same year, the 20th Century Theater became the home for the Cincinnati Church of Christ.

The movie theater remained the home for the church for four years before it decided to leave the building as well. The theater fell into different hands after the church left. In October 1997, the building became a popular venue in the area. Musical bands from across the country sometimes stop at the 20th Century Theater to play. Weddings and other events are also held here. Finally, the history of the theater was able to come full circle and hold performances again.

With such an eclectic history, it is no wonder that the place has gained the reputation for having ghosts on site.

The most famous ghost from the theater is that of an old projectionist. The story goes that during the days when the 20th Century was still showing movies, there was an older man who was working as the projectionist. Apparently he had been working as a projectionist for most of his life and had worked at the 20th Century for most of those years.

In the days when he ran the projection booth, the film projectors could only hold about 20 minutes worth of film. What the projectionist would have to do was switch power back and forth between the two projectors in the projection booth after each 20 minutes would pass. They called this a reel change.

Once this particular projectionist was showing a film when suddenly the audience was shocked to realize that he had missed a reel change. Everyone knew the projectionist, and they knew that he never missed a reel change. One of his friends from the audience rushed up to the booth to find that the projectionist was lying on the floor. He had died from a heart attack during the film.

While the authors could not find any historical evidence to back this story and the theater's current management claims that the story of the projectionist is only a local legend, the projection booth is host to a variety of strange occurrences.

Footsteps are often heard from around the projection booth. When these footsteps are investigated, a source is never found. Sometimes when people are alone in the projection booth, they hear someone cough right beside them. When they look up to see who is sitting next to them and coughing, there is never anyone there. Sometimes, even today, people will hear what sounds like a movie projector running up in the booth, but when they go up there to check on the sound, the sound just fades away.

Once there was a man who came into the building with his two dogs. As soon as the man took the dogs up to the balcony area near the projection booth, the dogs began barking and howling uncontrollably. They seemed to be in a panic and tried their best to run off in different directions. These dogs had never acted like this before; it was as if something up there on the balcony of the theater had frightened them. Eventually the dogs were able to get free of the man and run howling out of the building. When the man went chasing after them, they were waiting for him calmly outside the building. They would not go back inside.

There are also strange occurrences that happen in the VIP room of the current 20th Century Theater. Today this room is a nice little lounge, complete with a bar and a pool table and several small tables. The room was once used for storage. This was where a lot of the projectionist's equipment was stored. So if the story of the projectionist who died in the booth was true, he could be responsible for the hauntings here as well.

Once a bridesmaid from a wedding being held at the theater was in the VIP room alone, waiting for the bride and other bridesmaids to arrive. As she sat in a chair near the bar in the room, she heard sounds coming from the room with the pool table. It sounded like someone was moving the mirror that was leaning up against the wall in the room. Thinking that she was alone, she decided to get up to check on the noise. She found that there was no one in the room and nothing seemed to be out of place.

As she was looking in the poolroom for the source of the sound, though, she heard the door to the VIP area open. She went out to see who was there and again saw nothing. There was no one at the door or even outside the door.

In this room, people will report strange noises all the time. They cannot explain where the noises come from, and even through investigation they are never able to find the source. They will hear things like voices and footsteps, but upon further investigation, they find that there is nothing there.

Whatever the source of these ghostly occurrences, they always seem to happen during off times. Nothing ever seems to happen during a performance or an event. If the ghost is that of the projectionist, he knows that his job is to make sure that the performance goes on without interruption.

The 20th Century Theater is not the only haunted building in the immediate area. Right across the street from the theater is a building that is older than the theater itself. Originally, in the early 1900s, the building was called Luke's Lounge. Today it is called Habit's Café.

Luke's Lounge was a popular bar throughout most of the 1900s. In the 1940s, there were allegedly several illegal operations going on within the bar. One operation involved the owner of the bar fencing stolen merchandise with the help of a police officer. When the officer was fatally shot in the basement of the lounge, the owner was a suspect in the murder since he had known mafia ties and had already amassed a series of burglary convictions. He was not convicted for the

This photograph shows the basement of Habit's Café. Habits Café is a relatively small but cozy café that offers food, drinks, and spirits for its guests. During normal business hours, the basement is off limits to anyone but employees. In order to protect their insurance rates, the owners do not allow patrons in the basement. The basement is large and contains many different rooms. According to the management, it is very easy to get lost while walking around the different rooms. At the end of the short hallway shown in this photograph, a manager at Habit's saw the apparition of a man wearing a white zoot suit.

crime, however. Several weeks later, a family member of the owner was found shot to death in an alley near the bar.

Since most of the hauntings today at Habit's Café occur in the basement of the building, many people trace the ghosts back to the murder of this police officer.

Once Mark Rogers, the owner of Habit's Café, was in the basement with a couple of other people doing maintenance work. They were in the basement, cleaning the place up and painting the walls. Without any kind of warning or trigger, all the men in the basement suddenly felt uncomfortable. They all got chills down their spines and had the unshakable feeling that they were being watched. They even mentioned this feeling to one another, and they all admitted that they felt the same way.

As all the men continued to work in the basement of the then empty building, they started hearing footsteps in the room all around them even though none of them were walking around. They looked through the basement to find out where these footsteps were coming from, but they were the only people there. These footsteps seemed to have no source. Perhaps they were being made by whatever invisible entity was watching them as they worked just minutes earlier.

Another series of ghostly occurrences happened during filming of a movie called *April's Fool*. It was a film noir gangster film, and several scenes were shot in Habit's Café.

Things were going fine with the shoot until the production moved into the basement of the building. At this point, things began to get weird. They started having all kinds of technical problems as soon as they moved into the basement. Many of the monitors that they were using did not work in the basement. Sometimes the sound would not even record. Technical difficulties were beginning to put strain on the entire shoot.

The actors who were playing gangsters in the film would seem to cause even more problems with the equipment. The sound would not record, there would be problems with the cameras, and there would be problems with the lights and other electrical equipment. Eventually they had to give up on getting good takes for some of the scenes that were shot with these actors in the basement.

Another time during the filming, the crew saw a glowing ball of light materialize in the basement and begin to bounce around. They were filming at the time, so they assumed that they would be able to see the ball of light on the film when they reviewed it later. Even though everyone who was there that day saw the ball of light, there was nothing on the screen when they reviewed the film.

Once Aaron Rokoe, the general manager of the building, walked down into the basement for some reason or another and had his own experience with the haunted building. He walked into the basement and saw a man wearing a white zoot suit and a white fedora standing in the corner in the basement. When the man in the 1940s zoot suit looked up and made eye contact with Aaron, the man ran away. Aaron looked for him but found no sign of him anywhere in the building. He simply vanished. Neither of them said a word.

Whether it is the ghost of a projectionist or a murdered police officer, strange things seem to happen from time to time in these two buildings that sit across Madison Avenue from one another in Oakley. During peak times, these two buildings seem almost normal, like any other such building in the area, but once people are alone or away from the daily grind of these businesses, weird and unexplainable things begin to occur. Are the witnesses hallucinating or misinterpreting some natural thing, or are the spirits of those men who have passed away in these buildings occupying these rooms eternally?

Camp Dennison: The Lone Soldier

War is a terrible thing. It is traumatic to everyone involved. People rush into battle for fleeting causes and kill one another in this act of brutal savagery. Luckily, the North American continent

This is a photograph of the cemetery near Camp Dennison in Indian Hill. It is known as the Waldschmidt Cemetery and was used during the Civil War as a burial place for more than 300 Union soldiers and for 31 Confederate prisoners of war. Once the Civil War ended and Camp Dennison was torn down, many of the bodies of these soldiers were moved. The Union soldiers were moved to Spring Grove Cemetery in Cincinnati while the Confederates were moved to Camp Chase in Columbus. The soldiers who were buried here still haunt the cemetery grounds. Many times people will hear screams when they walk through the cemetery at night. Others will see shadowy figures dressed as Civil War soldiers walking among the headstones.

has not seen many wars take place on its soil. Southwestern Ohio has seen even less military action within its 200-year history.

That is not to say that southwestern Ohio is completely immune to the horrors of war. During the late 1700s and early 1800s, many battles with Native Americans happened in and around the area. Then, of course, there was the Civil War. While not much actual fighting occurred in the area, the horrors of that terrible war did leave their mark on southwestern Ohio.

Not too many Cincinnatians know that there was a famous Civil War training camp in Cincinnati. Even fewer know where it was or what occurred in those fields.

In April 1861, Civil War broke out in America. South Carolina and other southern states were beginning to break away from the United States. Pres. Abraham Lincoln was unwilling to allow the Union to dissolve without a fight, so he called the loyal northern states to arms. The war would drag on for longer than four years and result in the most battle casualties ever on American soil.

When the war started, no one was quite sure which states would secede to the Confederacy. Since Kentucky was a slave state, many Ohioans were afraid that Kentucky would leave the Union. This would make the Ohio River the boundary between the north and south. This would make Cincinnati a big city that sat right on the front lines of the war.

Gen. George McClellan, a man who would lead the Army of the Potomac and later run against Lincoln for the presidency of the United States, decided that it would be militarily prudent to set up a training camp for Union soldiers in Cincinnati. Since the war might start in Cincinnati, General McClellan wanted a suitable force stationed there in case it was attacked.

Near the end of April 1861, the site was chosen for the training camp. It was a large flat tract of land just north of Cincinnati in an area known as New Germany. There was enough flatland to have proper space to drill, and it was near the rail lines. Trains could easily take the troops to the front lines of battle whenever the need arose.

McClellan named the site Camp Dennison in honor of Ohio's governor. William Dennison had provided the funding needed to get the camp started. With all the logistics in place and the plans for the camp laid down, recruits started pouring into the camp from all over Ohio.

Things did not begin well for the camp. While on paper the camp seemed like it would operate properly, many things went wrong in the beginnings of the camp.

The spring of 1861 was unusually rainy. Most of May was overcast and wet, and as the regiments began to move into the camp, they were forced to build their own shelters and barracks. May was spent trying to build flimsy board structures in the rain. While everyone in these early months was a volunteer, the rain and their substandard barracks immediately hurt their morale.

All they had to eat at the camp was rice, potatoes, and bacon. All they had to drink besides water was coffee. The commanders of the camp required the cooks to be picked from the recruits themselves. A lot of the men had little or no experience with cooking since their wives or mothers had done the cooking throughout most of their lives. As a result, the food was oftentimes terrible. Sometimes it was even inedible.

Luckily, the patriotic women from Cincinnati would oftentimes travel up to the camp and bring food for the troops. So occasionally, the troops were able to get a meal that would actually satisfy them.

The water that was provided was no better for the troops. The company that pumped and provided the water for the troops got the water from the river that ran alongside the camp. The slaughterhouse at the camp would dump its refuse into the river, and the recruits themselves would oftentimes relieve themselves into the river. The water was retrieved downstream from the camp, so all the refuse from the slaughterhouse and from the soldiers would end up back in the drinking water.

This picture depicts what is today a bike trail that runs alongside the grounds of Camp Dennison in Indian Hill. Train tracks once ran along the same path as this bike trail. The trains that ran along these tracks could quickly transport troops from the Civil War–era camp to the battlefield. After the Civil War ended, the entire camp was razed and the land was returned to its original owners. The train tracks fell into disuse and were eventually torn up and replaced with the bike trail shown here. Today the ghost of a Civil War soldier reportedly haunts this bike trail. A man dressed in a Civil War uniform is often seen along this path. He always vanishes into thin air when someone approaches him.

The building depicted here is the Waldschmidt house. This building stood during the area's use as an army training camp in the 1860s. The house and the nearby Waldschmidt barn were both essential to the operation of the camp. The Waldschmidt house was used as the headquarters of the commandant of the camp. The nearby barn was originally used as a hospital. When the camp was first established, it was incredibly rainy and wet. Since the rain left no opportunity to build any permanent structures at the camp, many of the men fell ill. This required that the Waldschmidt barn be used as a hospital for those who were sick. Later in the war, more hospital buildings would be built throughout the camp. The original barn and hospital buildings have since been torn down. The house is the only building that was used in this area during the Civil War that still stands to this day.

Eventually the soldiers protested against the dirty water and turned over any cart of water that came from downstream. The pumping station was moved upstream from the camp because of this. Also, more permanent restrooms were constructed so that the men would not use the river as a bathroom.

The Ohio soldiers themselves were far from disciplined. Many of them had come from families that had to blaze their own trail into the Ohio wilderness and make their own living off the land. They were not used to being in such an organized situation, and they had no experience taking orders or respecting authority. The troops held little or no respect for the officers in charge of the camp.

One story says that a general was hammering at night in order to tighten a loose door on his sleeping quarters. A new recruit walked up to him and started yelling at him. He said that he was trying to sleep and that the hammering was keeping him awake. When the recruit realized that the man hammering was a general, he apologized to the general. He said that he was sorry; he said that he thought the general was just some captain.

Soon, though, as the men fell into the routine of camp life and the officers came up with new and better methods of training and control, life began to get easier at Camp Dennison. Out of the camp came perhaps the best fighting regiment in the Union army, the Ohio 9th. The Ohio 9th was a German regiment from Cincinnati that was renowned for its discipline and skill. The regiment was ready to fight after only a short time of training and was a deciding force in many of the largest battles of the war.

After the Battle of Shiloh, at the time the bloodiest battle on the North American continent, wounded troops began pouring into the Cincinnati area for treatment. Military hospitals were set up on the western edge of Camp Dennison, and many of the wounded Ohio and Indiana soldiers throughout the rest of the war would end up in these hospitals.

Unfortunately, though, treatment and medicine were not good in the middle 1800s. If a wound in a leg was infected, the doctors would oftentimes just saw it off. Many times they would saw off many limbs with the same hacksaw and would never wash the saw off.

Thousands of soldiers died in the hospitals there at Camp Dennison throughout the course of the war. The *Cincinnati Enquirer* would print daily lists of those who died at Camp Dennison. These lists were always long, and they never seemed to stop coming.

A cemetery was constructed near the camp where many of the bodies from the hospitals could be buried. Some of the bodies were unknown and were buried without any indication of who they were. They would be forced to lie there throughout eternity in anonymity.

Also there was a battle that occurred very near Camp Dennison. Gen. John Hunt Morgan from the Confederacy took his cavalry unit from Kentucky into the north in 1863. He crossed the Ohio River into Indiana and slowly wreaked havoc as he moved eastward toward Cincinnati.

To slow his approach, Gen. Ambrose Everett Burnside from Camp Dennison, charged with the defense of Cincinnati, destroyed the bridge at the Great Miami River at Miamitown, forcing Morgan's Raiders to cross farther north. This forced General Morgan to pass just north of Camp Dennison.

General Morgan could see the camp from where he passed it. There were far too many soldiers there for General Morgan to do anything but run. Still, Camp Dennison sent some troops up to attack Morgan's Raiders, slowing them down with several bloody skirmishes near Camp Dennison. Eventually General Morgan was caught, and the remainder of his troops, those who had not died through the skirmishes or just through pure exhaustion, were imprisoned.

The camp continued training soldiers throughout the rest of the war. The hospitals continued to take in the wounded and do what they could for them for the rest of the war. By 1865, the war was coming to a close. Gen. Robert E. Lee of the Confederacy had surrendered in April 1865 at Appomattox Court House in Virginia, and only a few more skirmishes were occurring throughout the south.

By September 1865, the war was completely over and the south had lost. Since there was no longer a need for Camp Dennison and people from all over the country were ready to start forgetting the horrors of the war, they shut the camp down.

All the buildings were dismantled. The wood that was used for the buildings was sold off as scrap. Every trace of the encampment was torn up and sold off. Soon nothing was left except for the flatlands that were once used for the countless military drills and the cemetery that sat just south of the main road.

The land itself was returned to the farmers from which it was purchased. To further wipe any memory of this place off the land, the farmers plowed the land and planted crops on it. Today there is hardly any sign that this land used to be the famous Civil War training ground except for a simple bronze plaque, which states its historical significance.

Beyond that, only the spirits of the thousands who trained and died here remember what occurred on these grounds.

Today the railroad tracks that once passed adjacent to the camp are gone. No sign of them remain. On the land through which the tracks once passed there is now a bike trail. The bike trail stretches on for the length of the camp, ending at a residential street on the other side.

A huge expanse of flatland now stretches out in the Camp Dennison area. Most of the lands are today just a large grassy field. A road and a parking lot jut into the field.

The grounds are reputed to be haunted to this day.

Just past dusk, a woman was walking alone down the bike trail. As she moved farther and farther down the trail in the dimming sunlight, she saw a man standing alone farther up the trail. He was not moving, simply standing there, staring off toward the grounds of the camp.

As she approached closer to him, she noticed that he was dressed very strangely. He was dressed in a Civil War uniform, complete with blue jacket and blue hat. The woman assumed that this man was dressed for some reenactment or for something else having to do with the Civil War–era camp next to the trail, so she planned to ask him about it when she got close enough to him to speak to him.

But when she walked closer, the man began to dissipate and slowly disappeared before her eyes. By the time she reached the spot where he was standing, there was no trace of him remaining.

She was not the only one to see a man dressed in a Civil War uniform standing on the bike trail at Camp Dennison. Often people will report very similar stories. They will see a man in uniform standing on the trail, or they will see a man in uniform walking away from them. This figure that they see will always appear at night or just as the sun is going down, and the figure will always vanish just before the witness gets close enough to see any detail in the figure's face.

The flat grassy grounds of the camp itself are reputed to be haunted as well. People will sometimes hear voices at night coming from all around the grounds. Voices that sound like people yelling something unrecognizable are heard echoing across the fields. Sometimes those yells sound more like screams. These sounds never have an easily discernible source. There is no one walking through the fields yelling, and no matter where one walks throughout the camp, the voices still seem to echo from all around.

Sometimes there are even ghostly buildings that appear in the fields. Once a woman was driving through the area at night and she saw far off in the field what looked like two buildings that were covered in fog. She could see the windows of the building lit up dimly through the fog and thought that the buildings looked strange for some reason that she could not put her finger on.

The next day she drove through the same area during the day and looked out to where she had seen the buildings. The field was completely empty; there were no buildings out there at all.

The cemetery that sits just across the main road from the camp is also supposedly haunted. People will again hear screams and yelling echoing from all around them as they are in the cemetery at night. Also people will see shadowy figures dressed in Civil War uniforms walking through the cemetery at night, only to watch them disappear without a trace.

Many men from Civil War times spent the most traumatic years of their lives at this camp. Many men died here, unimaginably painful deaths. Most people from Cincinnati do not even know about this Civil War camp that existed through those turbulent years.

But for those who still pass by this area at night and for those who still walk these grounds alone, soldiers to whom this place was their life continue to haunt this area to this day.

Eight

BUTLER COUNTY

Some riddles are better left unanswered. Terrible things will sometimes happen in the most unassuming neighborhoods at the most unassuming times. People who were "a good neighbor" or "a nice guy" will show themselves capable of the most brutal of acts. A "safe neighborhood" in a "good part of town" can sometimes play host to the most horrible scenes imaginable. A day of "reverence," "happiness," and "celebration" can become one of the most terrifying days of recent memory.

When things like this happen, when the comfortable world in which people live gets turned on its head, when something more terrible than even the most vivid dreams could possibly portray occurs, one can only ask why. One asks why, but does one truly want to know the answer?

Maud Hughes Road: The Screaming Bridge

Liberty Township reeks of history. Fields seem to stretch out forever, stretching westward toward an uncertain frontier. Some of the old farmhouses and schoolhouses seem much the same as they were as the town grew around the old stagecoach route that gave it life. Now the rails of the Norfolk Southern carry life from the town's heart.

On an inconsequential road on the eastern side of the town there is a haunted bridge that spans these tracks—that has spanned these tracks since the days when the Short Line Railroad traversed these ancient rails.

The bridge is part of a wooded section of Maud Hughes Road that is sparsely populated by residential homes. It crosses the tracks at an S in the road. All one can see of the road is heavy foliage at every corner. But this is sharply contrasted when one looks off the bridge. Looking off the bridge is like looking into a different world. The view extends down the tracks where one can see what seems like forever. The parallel lines of the rails meet at the horizon.

Forest meets civilization; asphalt meets rails. One feels like an anachronism; the bridge is timeless.

The locals call it the Screaming Bridge. Historically it achieved this name because its metal decking would seem to scream as cars rolled across it. Traditionally, though, it gained this name because the screams of those who died here still haunt it. Today stone and asphalt have replaced the old metal decking of its original construction, but with the locals, it has retained its macabre name.

It is said that if one pauses at the bridge late at night, one can sometimes see trainmen walking along the tracks, seemingly lost within the darkness. They never say anything. They never take any notice of anyone or anything that passes; they just walk tirelessly down the endless tracks and disappear into the chill night air.

Legends say that these trainmen are the ghostly remnants of railroad employees who died in train accidents that occurred near the bridge. Also, it is said that sometimes a caboose is seen sitting dormant along the tracks. Soon the phantom caboose disappears without any indication that it was ever there.

Others say that the bridge is haunted by the several suicides that have happened there. One legend speaks of a woman who became pregnant before getting married—something that was

Many train accidents have occurred between the Screaming Bridge at Maud Hughes Road and the train station at Gano. Gano is on the southern end of West Chester Township and is part of the rail line that leads from Cincinnati through Hamilton. The New York Central train seen here is traveling north from Gano nearing the Maud Hughes Bridge. In 1909, a Big Four train traveling north from the Gano station along this same stretch of track met with tragedy. For some reason, the boiler on the train suddenly exploded, scalding the engineer and brakeman to death. An investigation into the accident showed that the boiler was in good condition and there was no reason that it should have exploded. Men dressed as railroad employees are seen walking the tracks underneath the Screaming Bridge at night, only to mysteriously vanish before onlookers' eyes. (Courtesy of the Dan Finfrock collection.)

Just south of the Screaming Bridge, near the northern border of West Chester Township, was a small train station known as Mauds Station. Mauds Station is pictured here. In 1976, a northbound train passed Mauds Station toward the overpass at Maud Hughes Road. A southbound train carrying long rails passed the bridge at the same time. Some of the rails on the southbound train had come loose and crashed through the front car of the northbound train, killing the engineer and injuring the brakeman. Eventually Mauds Station was no longer needed along this rail line, so it was torn down. The site of the accident, underneath the Maud Hughes Road overpass, still echoes with memories of the accident. People will hear phantom screams and see ghostly railroad cars near the bridge. (Courtesy of the Dan Finfrock collection.)

unheard of in those days. In order to try to save her own reputation, she brought her newborn baby to the bridge and threw it to its death down to the train tracks. Then she hung herself, unable to deal with the guilt.

Another legend says that a pair of lovers were to meet on the bridge, but as the man reached the rendezvous, he found his lover had hung herself off the bridge. He killed himself shortly thereafter. Stories say that his screams and her sobs can still be heard if one waits at the bridge late at night.

Once a group of teenagers were hanging out underneath the bridge. As they were down there, they heard some kind of commotion on top of the bridge as if there was someone walking around up there. Suddenly they heard someone jump off the bridge and saw dangling legs hanging over the side of the bridge. It appeared as if someone had just hung herself off the bridge. The teenagers rushed to the top of the bridge to see what had happened and to see if they could save the lady. When they got to the top of the bridge, there was no sign that there was anyone there. When they went back below the bridge to see the dangling legs, they were gone.

Many people report hearing sourceless voices carry on entire conversations within earshot. Many more report hearing those phantom screams that have given the bridge its legendary name. The whole area screams with the torment of all those who suffered here.

Oftentimes, when evaluating the history of events like those stories behind these hauntings, it is difficult to separate myth from fact. This is especially true when looking into suicides. The reason that it is so difficult to locate historical evidence of suicides is that people who committed suicide were considered to have committed a mortal sin and were not permitted to be buried in consecrated ground. To many people of the time, this meant that the souls of these people would have to suffer an eternity in hell, and the families of those suicides would be forced to live out the remainder of their lives with the shame of this.

So if friends or family discovered that someone had committed suicide, often the facts of the incident would be hidden. Often authorities would officially document the death as an accident, and the reputation of those involved would be saved.

But this is not necessarily the only reason that historical evidence of suicides on the bridge is suspiciously absent. Oftentimes in isolated areas like this bridge, local people will embellish or simply make up stories. The stories will somehow take on a life of their own and evolve of their own volition as they are passed from person to person. When the legend is finally recorded, it has become a kind of urban myth, a fictional story with only very loose connections to fact. It is possible that the stories of the girl killing her baby and then herself or the lovers who killed themselves on the bridge are nothing but urban myths.

Although there is no documented proof of suicides occurring on the bridge, the bridge itself has seen its share of death and tragedy. Perhaps the most horrific of these tragedies occurred on October 4, 1909. What happened was a Big Four train was traveling down the tracks near the bridge at Maud Hughes. Suddenly the boiler exploded, toppling the train on the tracks and pinning engineers Charles Wikoff and Oscar Pease underneath the wreckage. They attempted to scream and escape, but they were scalded to death by boiling water from the boiler. Other people on and near the train during the accident were scalded and seriously injured. Chaos erupted as the injured waited for help to arrive.

Within a half hour of the accident, help arrived at the scene. Screaming and cries of agony filled the air. Surgeons and doctors took the injured away in ambulances as quickly as they could, attempting to save who they could. The bodies of Wikoff and Pease were nearly unrecognizable as they still lay in the scalding water. As the wrecking train arrived to clean up the wreckage that was sprawled across 50 feet of track, people from all around the area came to watch. They stood atop the hills for eight hours as the wrecker worked to clear the remains of that Big Four train. Three more men would perish from injuries resulting from the accident.

There was an investigation done to find out what had caused the boiler to explode. Despite exhaustive searching, no reason was ever found as to why the boiler exploded. It was in almost perfect condition.

In June 1976, another accident occurred under the Maud Hughes Road overpass killing one man. On this particular morning, two trains were passing side by side on the tracks under the Screaming Bridge. One train was headed northbound, and another train was headed southbound. The southbound train was carrying long rails on flatbed cars. Unfortunately, the rails were not tied down tightly on one of these cars and the rails had shifted, pointing out the side of the train like a jouster's lance. The loose rail went through the first car of the oncoming northbound train, impaling James Findley, the engineer. Findley was killed instantly, and the brakeman next to him was seriously injured as the rails from the oncoming train crashed into the car and destroyed the generator. Findley's train continued 300 feet down the tracks before finally stopping. Findley was the only fatality in the incident, but he was killed in a horrific manner.

Beyond these two train accidents there are many records of lives lost in automobile accidents on the bridge itself. Since the creation of the overpass, at least 36 people have died in automobile accidents on or near the bridge. Seven people were killed on the bridge over just a two-year span according to the Liberty Township board of trustees. The bridge itself was and still is a very dangerous place to traverse.

So while some of the stories behind the hauntings at the Screaming Bridge may be nothing more than urban legends, there are plenty of tragedies that actually occurred on this unassuming stretch of road that could easily account for the ghosts that haunt it. Perhaps the screams are the echoes of those scalded to death by the Big Four boiler explosion in 1909. Perhaps the ghostly figures are those trainmen who died here. Perhaps the sobs and the voices are a final attempt by those who died here to communicate their terror to the living.

Princeton Road: Phantom Hitchhiker

Princeton Road stretches for many miles, eastward and westward across the northern extensions of the Greater Cincinnati area. It runs through Liberty Township, intersecting Maud Hughes Road quite near the Screaming Bridge and goes even farther east than that. Westward, it runs past Rose Hill Cemetery and into the city of Hamilton itself. This western extent of the road is haunted.

The locals are the ones who can recount what happened on this road many years ago. No one is sure of the year. No one knew those involved. Everyone heard the story from someone who knew someone who was involved.

What happened was there was a high school student from Hamilton who was on her way to the prom. It was a wonderful and exciting time for her. She had the boyfriend of her dreams, the perfect dress, and the perfect evening planned. She had been looking forward to the event for weeks.

Unfortunately, something happened where her boyfriend was unable to pick her up and drive her to the prom. No one remembers why, but the plan was that he would meet her there. She would have to drive herself to the prom. Since she had already had the perfect evening all planned, she was upset by this sudden change of plans, but she soon got over it. She put on her dress and began driving. This was the evening that she had been waiting for her entire young life, and she was not going to let a little thing like driving arrangements ruin that.

When she left for the prom, a light rain had started. This was another bad sign. She was afraid that the rain would mess up her hair and ruin her dress, so she rushed to get into the car and out of the rain. The rain started coming down harder as she turned onto Princeton Road.

The rain came down so hard that it was difficult for her to see clearly as she moved down Princeton. She knew that she should go more slowly than she was because of the rain, but her prom was so important to her that she sped on so that she would not be late.

Then, suddenly, for one reason or another, she lost control of the car and crashed somewhere off the road. Perhaps she hit a puddle and lost control. Perhaps she swerved to avoid hitting an animal. No one knows exactly why she crashed that night.

Eventually another car passed on the road and saw her wrecked vehicle on the side of the road. The driver of the other car stopped to see whether the driver of the wrecked vehicle was all right. When he stepped up to the wreckage and looked into the driver-side window, he could see that he was too late. She was already dead.

She never made it to prom that night. But the legends go on to say that sometimes she still tries to make it.

A woman was driving down Princeton Road at night near Rose Hill Cemetery when she saw a young girl hitchhiking on the side of the road. The young girl looked well dressed and was very pretty. The woman driving the car stopped to pick her up because she was worried about the girl's safety. She did not feel a girl of that age should be hitchhiking; it was far too dangerous for her.

The girl thanked the woman for picking her up, and the girl sat next to the woman in the front seat of the car. The woman asked her where she was heading. The girl asked if the woman could take her to a building down the road a little ways. The woman knew the building that she was talking about. Since it was not too far out of her way, the woman decided to take the girl all the way there to save her from having to hitch the rest of her ride.

The girl was very quiet during the ride. Whenever the woman would ask her a question, she would give a very short answer. It seemed obvious that the girl did not want to talk, so the woman just left her alone.

After driving the girl down the road for a few miles, the woman suddenly felt a chill down her spine. She looked over to the passenger seat of the car. It was empty.

She had not stopped at any time since she had picked up the hitchhiker. The girl had simply vanished without a trace. The driver panicked. She had no idea what to make of what had happened, so she pulled over to the side of the road to collect her thoughts for a while.

As she sat there on the side of Princeton Road shaking with fear, a car passed her. The car that passed slammed on its brakes shortly after and skidded before slamming into a large tree branch that had fallen across the road.

The woman got out of her car to see if the driver of the other car was ok. She looked into the driver seat of the other car and the driver was unhurt, just dazed by the accident. He said that he would have hit the branch even harder if he had not seen her car stopped on the shoulder.

She explained the strange story of the hitchhiker that she picked up and about how the hitchhiker mysteriously disappeared. As she told the man the story, he turned white. He told the woman that he had seen the girl. He said that as he drove by Rose Hill Cemetery, a young girl was hitchhiking on the side of the road, but he decided not to pick her up.

While the stories about this apparition rarely report the ghost as appearing in the exact same spot, the ghost is always reported in the same general area of the road. Those who have been lucky enough to see this specter always seem to witness it on Princeton Road near Rose Hill Cemetery.

Here Princeton is somewhat secluded at night. The businesses near this area are all closed, so those driving down the road are alone. Several hundred yards to the south, the Michael A. Fox highway runs parallel to Princeton and into Hamilton. Only forests and farmland are to the north.

There are two stories that witnesses to this phantom hitchhiker report. The first story involves the vehicles that actually stop to pick up the hitchhiker. These stories always end the same. The phantom hitchhiker will tell the driver the destination that she wants to go to. As the driver is driving her there, they suddenly look over and see that the hitchhiker is no longer in the car. She has mysteriously vanished without a trace.

Most of the reports of the phantom hitchhiker traveling along Princeton Road state that she most often appears just outside of Rose Hill Burial Park. This photograph shows Princeton Road looking east from Rose Hill's driveway. This is the section of Princeton where the phantom hitchhiker is most often seen. The cemetery itself does not display any headstones, believing that the headstones may mar the overall beauty and tranquility of the place. Instead of headstones, flat metal plaques mark the burial places of the deceased. Without headstones to block out any of the view, the rolling hills and aesthetic foliage are clearly visible throughout the park. The cemetery itself is not haunted; it is instead peaceful and tranquil. For some reason or another though, many reports of the phantom hitchhiker from Princeton Road originate here, just outside of the cemetery gates, where the tranquility of the cemetery ends and the reality of the outside world begins.

The second story that goes along with this phantom is a little more frightening. These stories involve the vehicles that do not stop to pick up the hitchhiker. The driver sees the girl on the side of the road and decides against picking her up for whatever reason. The way that these stories always end is that the car ends up getting into an accident. Whether an animal jumps out in front of their car or a tree branch has fallen unseen across the middle of the road, those cars that do not pick up the hitchhiker always seem to meet with calamity on Princeton Road.

Some people claim that this girl serves as a warning to these vehicles. Since she herself was killed in a car accident on this road, she roams the road forever in an attempt to warn vehicles of upcoming danger. Perhaps even the sight of her has caused speeding vehicles on the road to drive just a little more carefully to avoid hitting any other hitchhikers that may be walking along the road ahead. Perhaps her ghost has saved lives.

Other people claim that this girl is not out to save these doomed vehicles. These other people think that the girl causes the accidents to those vehicles that do not pick her up. They think that she is angry that the vehicles are not going to take her to her prom, so she causes whatever tragedy is waiting for them down the road.

Butler County Fairgrounds: A Suicide

Only remnants of the day exist during the night. Only ghosts roam the abandoned fairgrounds. In the off season, on off days, when the fair has ended or has not yet begun, the large tract of flatland set off as the Butler County Fairgrounds stands in solitude. It is fenced off from the rest of the world. It is hollow. It is alone.

The grandstands look out toward an empty field. The blacktopped paths sit quietly, only touched as the occasional decaying leaf is carried across it by the wind. Booths that had once sold funnel cakes or ride coupons sit stripped and vacant. Nothing stares out from the darkness within the buildings.

Everything is silent. Everything seems to be waiting until the county fair brings this collection of depleted husks to life.

These fairgrounds date back to 1856, when the Butler County Agricultural Society purchased the land to suit its rapidly expanding county fair. By 1856, the Butler County Fair had become the highest-rated agricultural fair in the entire state of Ohio. Farmers would come from all over the state to show off their wares at the fairgrounds.

The fair was considered a farmer's holiday and would take place annually on the second week in October. It continues today on the same dates in October. The fair began with just a couple of wagons that would show off the latest farming technology. The farmers would also bring their best livestock and produce to sell and show off at the fair.

Over the years, the fair would expand exponentially. The first year that the fair took place, the fair made $320. In recent years, the fair has brought in more than $600,000 annually. Despite its humble beginnings as a few wagons and farmers, the fair has grown into its massive fairgrounds. There are permanent buildings and rides that have been constructed there over the years.

In 1876, the agricultural society set up a horse-racing track and grandstands in order to boost attendance at future fairs. The wood frame grandstands were a success, and the Butler County Fair far exceeded any other fair in Ohio in terms of attendance and profit. In 1913, a mysterious fire burned the grandstand to the ground. The fairgrounds were not in use at the time, so no one was hurt in the blaze. Later that year, though, the agricultural society decided to build a new grandstand that was made of concrete. This was to stop it from burning down again, but historically it became the first completely concrete grandstand in the United States. It still stands today as a testament to its durability.

Throughout the years, the fair has become bigger and bigger, making the fairgrounds the focal point of entertainment in Butler County during the second week in October. It is throughout

This is where Princeton Road dead-ends on its western edge. Next to this dead end, there is a church, and Rose Hill Cemetery lies less than a mile down the road. Also the haunted Butler County Fairgrounds are only a block south of this road. Legends say that it is somewhere between this dead end of the road and Rose Hill Cemetery that people will often see a young girl hitchhiking along the road. Supposedly she is the ghost of a young girl who was killed in an automobile accident on the way to her prom. The stories go that those who pick up the hitchhiker are startled when farther down the road they realize that the hitchhiker has vanished into thin air. Also this phantom hitchhiker seems to warn passing motorists of some danger in the road up ahead. Those who refuse to pick her up will often get into accidents on this road.

The grandstands at the Butler County Fairgrounds were built because of the rapidly growing fair. The Butler County Agricultural Society decided that the fair was becoming so popular that it needed a horse-racing track and grandstands to accompany it. The original grandstands were made completely of wood. In 1913, an accident caused the wooden grandstands to burn to the ground, and later that same year, construction was started on a more modern concrete grandstand at the same location. The new grandstand was constructed completely out of concrete and is believed to be the first concrete grandstand in the United States. The ghost of the fairground is reputed to walk out of the restrooms located behind these grandstands. The ghost is a man with a bullet wound in his head who mysteriously vanishes before onlookers' eyes. Legends say that he committed suicide in the restroom behind the grandstands. (Courtesy of the Butler County Historical Society.)

The Butler County Agricultural Society built the Butler County Fairgrounds in 1856. The first fair held at the Butler County Fairgrounds generated $320. The fair continued to do very well, constantly gaining more and more revenue and eventually became one of the highest-rated fairs in the state of Ohio. The only years that the fair did not generate a profit was during the Civil War. By 1868, it was nearly as popular as the state fair. Hundreds of people would show up for the various races on these tracks. These grounds once held plowing matches and horse races, and today it continues to hold similar events. The fair still sees an annual attendance of over 84,000 people and generates an excess of $536,000. Today the fair has games, rides, livestock exhibits, and other popular attractions, attracting all types of people and cultures.

the rest of the year, when the hustle and bustle of the fair has died down and the grounds become simply the empty shell of what they have the potential of becoming, that the ghosts of this area come out to play.

Amid these empty streets and buildings, a ghost walks only at night. Often people will report seeing this apparition walking dejectedly from booth to booth, through the walkways, and through the grandstands.

Once someone was walking near the fence at the outskirts of the fairgrounds at night. He glanced over into the empty grounds and saw a man walking around from building to building. The figure seemed to have an aura around him. Although most of the fairgrounds were quite dark, a very light glow seemed to follow the figure around as he walked. Eventually the figure glanced up at the man by the fence and then slowly dissipated into the night.

Another time a group of people was cleaning up the fairgrounds during the immediate aftermath of the fair. A handful of workers were dispersed throughout the grounds and a man was working near the restrooms at the concrete grandstands. As he casually worked to clean up the area near the grandstands, the door to the men's restroom opened up and a man walked out. The employee figured that the figure was one of the other employees who had just wandered into the area to use the restroom, but as the man looked closer at the figure exiting the bathroom, he did not recognize the person.

The figure slowly began to turn toward the employee. To his surprise, the man had a gunshot wound to his face. He was missing his right eye, and blood flowed freely down his face. The employee stepped back in horror as the man with the gunshot wound began to slowly disappear into the night.

These are not the only encounters with this man from the fairgrounds. Encounters with this ghost will often involve a detailed description. He is often reported to have suffered a gunshot wound to the head. Despite the wound, he still walks purposefully from booth to booth and around the entire fairgrounds, disappearing when approached, never acknowledging interaction from any of the living.

Locals have developed legends about where this ghost originated. One day during the fair, a lonely man entered the restroom there at the fairgrounds. In that restroom, he shot himself in the head. He died there.

The Butler County Historical Society has no record of such a suicide occurring during one of the fairs there. Oftentimes, though, in the late 1800s and early 1900s, suicides were covered up to save the reputation of those who were involved. Suicide cases would shame the ones who committed the act and their families so they are often listed in the official records as accidents. Perhaps the suicide in the fairgrounds restroom did historically occur, but its proof has been lost to history.

Whether or not this man actually killed himself in the restroom here is inconsequential though; he still refuses to stop wandering the fairgrounds long into the dead of night.

The Ruppert House: Mass Murder on Minor Avenue
In 1975, the house looked the same. It looked no different than the other houses along the street. It had white siding, a window upstairs, a front yard, and a mailbox hanging slightly crookedly underneath the three-digit address: 635.

Before April 1975, the house was normal. The house was just like every other house; it was lost among the simplicity of life.

But then something awful happened there. Something happened that no one could possibly have foretold, something that haunts the entire city of Hamilton to this day.

But to fully understand what terrible events led to this house being one of the most famous haunted houses in the city of Hamilton, one must start from the beginning. The story begins when James Ruppert was just a boy.

James Ruppert was not much like the other boys his age. His family lived in a small house that had no running water. His father raised chickens in the back of the house, but this aggravated the boy's asthma condition. James suffered serious respiratory reactions to feathers and dust. His childhood home had plenty of it.

Because of his asthma, James was always sickly and was unable to participate in many physical activities. He could not play sports, and he was not allowed to attend gym classes. He would always walk hunched over from the sickness that he was constantly feeling.

James's father did not help to get James through these tough years of his life. James's father would constantly put him down and tell him that he was never going to be anything in life. He told James that he would never be able to hold down a job and that he would never be able to support himself.

James's early life was terrible. He was physically crushed by the asthma, but perhaps more dreadfully, he was put down by all those around him. He was teased constantly at school, and he would then come home to a clearly disappointed family. While this kind of childhood may be enough to haunt anyone into adulthood, things would soon get much worse.

When James was 12, his father died from tuberculosis. This left his mother and his brother Leonard in charge of the household. His mother became much worse than his father ever was. She would often beat him and tell him that he was a mistake. She would tell him that she had wanted him to be a girl. She told him how proud she was of Leonard, the successful athletic son who stepped up and helped out when his father died. She told James how disappointed she was in him and what he had become. She encouraged Leonard to beat him whenever he wanted as well. Leonard would lock him in closets, beat him with a belt, and sit on his head until he could not take it anymore.

James was so crushed by all this that he tried to hang himself with a bedsheet to end this misery. But he failed at that too. He survived his suicide attempt just to be yelled at and beaten for trying to kill himself.

Leonard would grow up and graduate college as an engineer. James would flunk out after only a couple of years of college. Leonard would marry and have eight children. James's only girlfriend would end up cheating on him and leaving him. Leonard was, at least in his mother's eyes, the success of the family, and James was the failure in every way.

By the time the family moved to the house on Minor Avenue in Hamilton, Leonard had moved and bought his own house with his wife and children. James was forced to live alone in the house with his mother. He could never hold down a job and was constantly without any money. Again he would constantly hear about his shortcomings from his mother.

By 1965, James's mind was on the verge of cracking. The Hamilton Police accused him of making an obscene telephone call to an employee at the local library. James felt that his family had told them that he had done that. James then began to feel that everyone was out to get him. He already knew that his mother and brother were out to get him, but now he thought that the FBI was tapping the telephones of every place that he frequented. He thought that the highway patrol was following him everywhere. He became incredibly paranoid. He was even convinced that his brother would sabotage his car whenever James turned his back.

It was around this time that James decided that he would buy a gun. He got a handgun, and with a little bit of practice, he finally found something that he was good at. He became a good marksman with a handgun, and he started to gather a collection of guns. He would go down to the Great Miami River and set a tin can down on the bank. He would then shoot the whole clip into the can, making it dance across the water. With the guns, James finally felt masculine. After being beaten down and teased for being so weak for most of his life, the guns made him feel like a man for the first time.

Today 635 Minor Avenue is identical to this 1975 photograph. Minor Avenue is a street with many houses with similar architectural styles running down each side. While many of the houses look identical, to the locals 635 is very different. On Easter Sunday in 1975, James Ruppert descended the stairs with several of his guns and executed every one of his 11 family members who had come to the house to celebrate the holiday. James Ruppert is currently in prison, but the spirits of those he killed are said to haunt the house to this day. Strange figures or sounds in the night are reported here, as well as dripping blood from the rafters in the basement ceiling. Strange things still happen in the house despite the fact that the grisly murders occurred almost 35 years ago.

But despite this small uplifting thing in his life, he still felt downtrodden by his family and felt stalked by law enforcement. Over the next 10 years, his insanity would build to a point where it could not be contained any longer.

In February 1975, James asked the owner of the store where he purchased his guns and ammunition where he could find a silencer. Come March, James's mother was threatening to kick him out of the house. He had been out of work for quite some time and was going out drinking every night. She told him that if he did not get a job, she was going to kick him out on the street.

Upset about this new obstacle in his life, worried that he was going to have to find a place to live when he had no money and no job, he went to his favorite bar to get a drink. He looked upset, and the waitress asked what was bothering him. He told her about the unemployment, his mother's constant nagging, and the possibility that he would soon be without a place to stay. He told the waitress that he had to take care of the problems as soon as he could. He left the bar but came back an hour or so later. The waitress asked him if he had taken care of his problems. He answered, "Not yet."

The next morning was Easter Sunday, and the whole family was coming to the house on Minor Avenue to celebrate the holiday. James's mother had been sick so Leonard, his wife, and his eight children decided not to come until later on in the afternoon so that she could get some much-needed rest. James himself was quite depressed. With the looming eviction and lack of income coupled with the holiday, James slept until almost 4:00 p.m.

James came downstairs as everyone was arriving for the party. He sat on the front porch to watch the eight children all go around the yard collecting Easter eggs. He chatted with his brother about politics for a while, and eventually everyone came into the house for dinner. James's mother was cooking sloppy joes, and suddenly he was overcome with depression again. He decided that the best way to get over his depression was to get out his guns and go down to the river and shoot for a while.

He grabbed his .357 Magnum, his two .22 handguns, and an 18-shot rifle and walked down into the kitchen. He rested his rifle up against the refrigerator and told Leonard and his mother that he was going down to the river to go shooting. His mother was at the stove. Leonard and his wife were sitting at the kitchen table. One of their daughters was in the bathroom, while another daughter waited impatiently by the bathroom door, waiting her turn. The other six children were playing in the living room.

Making casual conversation, Leonard said to James, "How's your Volkswagen, Jimmie?" James thought that this meant that Leonard had recently sabotaged his car. And then James snapped, and everything that had been building within his fragile psyche came pouring out.

After the comment about his car, James shot Leonard in the face with his .357. Leonard fell backward and onto the floor. Everyone else in the room was shocked. He then pointed the gun at Leonard's wife and shot her in the head. James's mother figured out what was going on and attempted to run at James to save the rest of her family, but he shot her dead before she could reach him.

Then he killed the children. He shot them all one by one. He even stopped so that he could reload. Not one of the children attempted to escape. Despite them seeing their brothers and sisters being shot dead in front of them, no one tried to hide or to save themselves. By the time he was finished, he had killed all 11 of his family members in the house. He had shot 10 of them in the head and 1 in the chest. He added two more bullets to each body to make sure that they were dead.

James had murdered more of his own family members than anyone else in history. To this day, Easter Sunday 1975 in the house at 635 Minor Avenue holds the record for the largest family mass murder in history.

Three hours later, James called the police. He said, "There's been a shooting here" and then hung up. The police arrived soon after. James opened the front door for the police and did not resist arrest. The police saw the bodies scattered around the kitchen and the living room. They were perplexed that there was absolutely no sign of a struggle. No one even displayed any defensive wounds.

The next day, Hamilton erupted into a media frenzy. Everyone wanted to know what had happened. Everyone wanted to know every little detail. No one who knew James could believe that he could do something like this. He was always a very nice and polite guy who always seemed to get along with his mother. One friend of the family to this day refuses to believe that James committed the murders, despite his confession, his motive, his presence at the scene, and his bloody fingerprints sprawled out across the house.

Over the next few days, hundreds of people would congregate on the front lawn of the Ruppert house to see the scene of the terrible crime. Minor Avenue became a morbid gallery for the curious. Everyone wanted to see the place where the terrible murders had happened.

A year later, the items in the house were all auctioned off. Hundreds of people came and bid for their chance to own a macabre souvenir of the murders. People searched for furniture or items from the house that were bloodstained. They knew that these items would be worth more money to collectors in the future. Soon everything in the house had been sold, leaving the house just a shell.

James himself went to court for the murders. He pleaded insanity. His defense was that his terrible childhood had caused his mind to become paranoid. The paranoia built over the rest of his life and finally came to a head that Easter Sunday. The defense said that this breakdown was inevitable, that it would have happened sooner or later no matter what. They argued that he belonged in a mental asylum, not a prison.

The prosecution argued that he committed the murders for money. He was the only surviving member of the family, so all the Ruppert family assets would revert to him. His brother had a nice house and a nice life insurance policy. His mother had a decent amount of money as well. The prosecution argued that James was upset that he was going to be evicted and had no money of his own, so he felt that this was the only way that he could hold onto enough money to keep the house.

They argued that turning himself in was all part of his plan. If he were convicted of murdering his family, he could not collect any inheritance by law. But if he was found not guilty by reason of insanity, the small fortune would revert to him, the only living Ruppert.

The prosecution won, and James was sentenced to two life sentences back to back. He is currently serving out his term at the Allen Correctional Institute in Lima. His next parole hearing will not be until 2035.

The house passed into other hands. Stories say that some people moved to Hamilton from out of town and were surprised to find such a good deal on the house on Minor Avenue. They had no idea what had happened in the house, and any remnants of that horrible day in 1975 had been removed. The stories go on to say that soon after, the people who moved into the house moved out. Locals say that something in that house scared them so much that they left without grabbing any of their possessions, and they never went back.

Others who have lived in that house since the incident have come back to tell stories of strange and eerie things that happen there from time to time. One man told the story of when he was a young boy living in the house. He was asleep in his bedroom with the door closed when for some reason or another he suddenly jolted awake. He looked around his dark room, suddenly very frightened for reasons he could not explain.

Then the light in the hallway came on, and he heard footsteps coming down the hallway toward his room. He was still frightened at this time but assumed that it was his mother walking down the hall to check on him. He saw someone stop in front of his bedroom door. He could see the silhouettes of the figure's two feet in the crack of light at the bottom of his door. The feet stood there for a second, and then without warning the hall light went off.

He got up quickly and ran out the door to see what his mother was doing, standing outside his door for so long. Also, he was still a little scared by the whole situation. He walked into his mother's room to find her fast asleep. There was no one else in the house.

Another past resident of the house reported having heard a sound from the upstairs hallway. She figured her son had awakened in the middle of the night and was walking around outside in the hallway. She decided to check on him and stepped out into the hallway. To her absolute horror, she saw a man standing in front of her son's room, looking into his open doorway. The man looked very colorless, but this lack of color could have been due to the poor lighting conditions. He looked like he had bags under his eyes and was generally haggard. All she knew is that she did not recognize him, and she immediately feared for her own safety and that of her child.

She screamed, but as soon as she screamed, the man vanished into thin air. She ran to the bedroom to find her son looking out toward the hallway with terror in his eyes. He had seen the figure as well.

Most other ghost stories about the house are from distant sources. Someone knew a guy who knew a guy who once lived in the house and he saw something strange. The most common story that comes out of this haunted house is the bloodstains in the basement. People say that sometimes at night the wooden joists on the ceiling start to drip blood down onto the basement floor.

Other people say that when alone upstairs, one can sometimes hear children playing downstairs in the living room, but upon investigation, the room is empty. Other people report that one can hear screams coming from inside the house late at night. Many times there are sourceless footsteps that walk all throughout the home.

James is still alive today. His next parole hearing will not be until he is 101 years old. But if he lives that long and does get his parole, where would he go? His only home has been taken, lived in by strangers and haunted by his victims.

A house with such a dark history is bound to generate rumors and urban myths. People are liable to create ghosts and stories from their imagination. It is possible that the ghost stories that surround this house are nothing but local imaginations running wild about this house where this terrible thing happened. On the flip side of this, though, if ever there was a house with reason to be haunted, 635 Minor Avenue would be that house.

This is an example of an apartment building on Front Street in Cincinnati. This photograph was taken in 1920, but the condition and appearance of these buildings is typical of what apartment buildings would have looked like on Front Street at the time of the Salvation Army fire in September 1900. In 1900, most people from Cincinnati lived downtown or in the immediate surrounding areas; cars and roads were not widespread enough to allow people to live far away from the heart of the city. The richest Cincinnatians lived just outside the city in neighborhoods like Mount Auburn and Price Hill, while the poorest Cincinnatians lived in tenements like those pictured here on Front Street. Eventually Front Street had garnered such a negative reputation among the people of Cincinnati that it was torn down. Over a period of a few decades, the entirety of Front Street, including those tenements depicted here, was demolished. New roads were eventually built where Front Street once ran, but they were no longer known as Front Street. (Courtesy of the Cincinnati Museum Center, Cincinnati Historical Society Library.)

Nine

CEMETERIES

Cemeteries are meant to be tranquil. They are meant to be peaceful places where the dead can rest in the beauty of nature for all eternity. Some cemeteries are able to capture this atmosphere quite effectively. In these places, the dead make no sound, and they stay hidden from the living. But they are always watching.

Weselyan Cemetery: The Salvation Army Fire

Weselyan Cemetery looks haunted. Every corner of the place, every tombstone, every hill, appears as if it were screaming in agony. It appears to be alive but tortured. It appears as some kind of a hell.

An unassuming headstone stands near the front of the cemetery at Colerain Avenue. The headstone is a two-foot-tall white obelisk next to a metal pipe that once flew a flag. The writing on the monument's face has worn off to a point where it is nearly impossible to read. At the top it says, "Dedicated to those who perished in the Salvation Army orphanage fire, September 17, 1900." Below this etching there are five names.

In 1900, the Salvation Army orphanage sat on Front Street. This area was one of the worst areas in town. It was infested by crime and was the home of those people who could not afford anywhere better. The children who lived in the orphanage were not really orphans, they were the children of those tenants of Front Street and lower Broadway who could not afford to stay home and care for their children. The parents of these children would go out into the city and work unrewarding factory jobs for most of the day before retrieving their children from the Salvation Army at 403 East Front Street.

The orphanage itself was in perhaps the most dangerous spot in the city. The orphanage was a three-story brick building, and it sat in the center of two of the most dangerous places in the city. On one side was Jo Fenton's saloon. Fenton's saloon was constantly the site of bar fights and murders. Drunkards would often get robbed of all they had as they stumbled out the doors of the saloon. Nowhere in the city was there a bar with a rougher reputation than Jo Fenton's.

On the other side of the orphanage were Terry Biggio's apartments. This building had a reputation for being as bad as Fenton's saloon. It was the definition of a slum. Nothing was kept clean or livable in the building, but the people who lived there could not afford to move anywhere else. The building had a reputation of housing prostitutes, thieves, and the worst scum who lived in the city at that time.

In September 1900, anyone who walked through the area could tell that there was gas leaking from somewhere in the neighborhood. The smell of the gas was strongest around the Biggio apartment complex, but no one in the area could afford to get the problem fixed. Everyone in the area just assumed that sooner or later someone would come and fix the problem, but no one ever did.

On September 17, all hell broke loose. It was a chilly day in Cincinnati, so the workers at the Salvation Army closed the doors and windows to keep in the heat. While it did succeed in keeping in the heat, it also caused the escaping gas from the neighborhood to build up in the building. Something sparked on the first floor, and a huge fire suddenly exploded on the bottom floor of the orphanage.

This photograph depicts an area known as "Rat's Row" on Front Street in Cincinnati. In the early 1900s, this area was considered by most to be the worst area in the entire city. The poorest people in the city with the worst jobs all lived in this part of town in terrible slums and broken-down apartment buildings. Many saloons and bars, like the Silver Moon (formerly Puckett's Saloon) pictured here, popped up along Front Street to help cater to those workingmen who would often want a drink after a long day at their low-paying jobs. Fights would break out at these saloons nightly. The fire at the Salvation Army orphanage in September 1900 occurred very near the area shown in this photograph. The orphanage was built in the worst part of town with the purpose to offer much-needed child care to those people who were out at work at all hours of the day. The entire area shown here was torn down in 1913. (Courtesy of the Cincinnati Museum Center, Cincinnati Historical Society Library.)

"Dedicated to those who perished in the Salvation Army orphanage fire, September 17, 1900" is engraved on this two-foot-tall obelisk. Also listed on the tombstone are the names of the five children who died in the Salvation Army fire on September 17, 1900. Listed are Maggie Williams, Edward Mullen, Myrtle Ferrell, Herbert Harkins, and Rhoda Harkins. Next to the obelisk stands a lonely metal pole. This pole once held the Salvation Army flag. This grave site is the possible origin of many of the hauntings at Weselyan Cemetery. In many of the stories, children laugh and play throughout the cemetery well after dark when the cemetery is closed. Sometimes children are heard screaming and crying. When the caretaker searches the cemetery, he can never find any sign of the children.

Captains Bertha Anderson and Elizabeth Erickson of the Salvation Army Corps were on the third floor with the 13 children from the house when the explosion ignited the first floor of the building. The fire started to spread rapidly. One newspaper account claimed that it seemed as if the walls had been soaked with oil.

Unfortunately for the workers and the children in the building, the stairs were the first thing to be eaten away by the fire. They were trapped. The stairs were their only avenue of escape. The children could only look out the third-story windows and decide how they were going to die, by fire or by a three-story fall to the pavement below.

Then something amazing happened. In the worst part of Cincinnati, in the most crime-infested and self-serving section that the city had ever seen, these criminals and riffraff became heroes. The people who the rest of the city had labeled scum and worthless risked their own lives to save the children they knew were trapped somewhere in the burning building.

People acted quickly as soon as they heard the gas explosion and realized the fire was at the orphanage. While many of the residents of the neighborhood stood around the front of the building, trying to figure out how they would save the children, Eddie Malloy and Willie Evans, 15-year-old children themselves, came up with a way to save them.

While most people were rushing down the stairs at Biggio's, Malloy and Evans rushed up the stairs and went up on the roof. Risking their own lives, they leapt from the roof of Biggio's to the roof of the burning Salvation Army building. They looked in through the skylight on the top floor of the orphanage and saw the frightened workers and children huddled in the room. They were able to bust out the skylight and save two children, which they carried down to safety.

A man named J. C. Wilson was a window cleaner who lived in Biggio's. He made sure that his wife and his own children were able to escape from Biggio's, then risked his life to go after the children in the orphanage. He climbed out his window and across to the third-floor window of the orphanage. He was able to grab three children and carry them back to his own window and down to safety. Wilson was seriously burned, but he would ultimately survive his injuries.

When the explosion happened, James Harkins was in his room at the close by Spencer Hotel. Harkins was unable to work since he had hurt his leg while working as a painter several months earlier, so he was in the room with six of his eight children while his wife was working at a home in Walnut Hills. His other two children, Rhoda and Herbert, were in the orphanage.

Without pausing, Harkins limped as fast as he could out of the Spencer and toward the burning orphanage. While the rest of the neighborhood watched helplessly as the children screamed on the third floor, Harkins limped straight into the burning building and up the burning stairs.

Seeing Harkins's bravery and fearing for his little sister Eva, a boy named Earl Bradford rushed into the burning building after Harkins. Since Bradford was not limping like Harkins was, he was able to run past Harkins on the stairs and grab the first child he saw. Bradford began to run back down past Harkins, but Harkins stopped him. He knew that Bradford could not make it back down the stairs with the child, so Harkins told him to go back down himself. Bradford was forced to roll down the stairs and was badly burned, but he would survive his injuries.

The child that Harkins took from him was his own daughter, Rhoda. He held her tight as he joined the rest of them in the burning third floor. At the last second a fire truck arrived at the scene and threw its ladder up to the third floor. Two more children were saved, but by that time, it was too late to save anyone else.

Firemen rushed into the building by the ladder and carried out as many bodies as they could. Harkins was dead from the flames, but his last-ditch effort to save his child had almost been successful. Rhoda was still breathing in his arms. She was badly burned, but she was still alive. They rushed her to the hospital.

Over the last couple decades, Weselyan Cemetery was allowed to deteriorate into an unfortunate state of disrepair. This marker shown here has almost been completely swallowed by the trunk of this large tree. Other facets of the cemetery were equally dilapidated. A mausoleum's stone doors were broken open displaying the coffins inside. Several trees around the cemetery had several broken headstones piled up around their bases. Other headstones had broken and were left on the ground where they fell. Recently, the cemetery has begun to make renovations to much of the grounds. Large piles of headstones no longer surround the base of trees, and the doorway to the mausoleum has been repaired. The headstone pictured here was unable to be salvaged though—it is still being slowly overcome by the trunk of the tree.

Both of the Salvation Army captains were killed in the fire. Out of the 13 children who were in the building, 8 were saved. Among those who survived without permanent injury was Eva Bradford, Earl Bradford's little sister.

The five who died are listed on the white tombstone in Weselyan Cemetery, next to the empty flagpole that once carried the Salvation Army flag: Maggie Williams, Edward Mullen, Myrtle Ferrell, Herbert Harkins, and despite doing all they could at the hospital, the final name on the list was that of poor Rhoda Harkins. Despite all his efforts and heroism, both of James Harkins's children perished in the fire. These children haunt this cemetery.

Most reports of activity coming from the cemetery after hours are reports of children beyond the fence. Sometimes people will hear children's laughter and children's voices playfully conversing with one another. Sometimes the caretaker himself will hear this laughter and assume that some children have broken into the cemetery after hours. He will investigate the entire cemetery and find no evidence of children anywhere. Oftentimes the laughter will seem to follow him as he roams the cemetery looking for trespassers, and he will even see what look like the shadows of children running from one tombstone to another. When he looks closer, though, there is nothing there.

Other times, people will hear the sounds of children crying out for help or screaming in terror. The people who hear it, whether a passerby or the caretaker himself, are certain that the screams came from within the cemetery. Upon further investigation, though, there are no children in the cemetery.

Perhaps these sounds are ghosts from the Salvation Army fire, forever forced to live and play within these cemetery gates.

But the fire is not the only aspect of the cemetery that could cause the dead to awaken. The state of the cemetery itself is reason enough for the spirits of those buried here to become angry at the living.

Several tombstones have been swallowed within the trunks of large trees. The mausoleums are all broken and dilapidated. One mausoleum has completely collapsed, revealing an opening into its dark interior. As people peer into the broken structure with a flashlight, chills ride down their spines as they half expect the long-departed resident to rise up and grab their wrists. They can almost feel the mausoleum's pain, if it could in fact feel pain.

The broken remains of many other tombstones are scattered about the cemetery. Some broken pieces, containing important names and dates of the dead, are thrown haphazardly into a pile near the base of an ancient tree.

Many of the other tombstones that still appear to be in their proper place are illegible. The writing has worn off their faces, and the deceased below will have to live in anonymity for eternity.

Cemeteries are meant to be places where the dead can rest, but can anyone rest in conditions such as these? Beyond the strange children who haunt the cemetery, other strange ghosts reside here. Often at night, people will report seeing dark silhouettes running through the cemetery. Screams and moans are also reported from within the gates of the cemetery after nightfall. The ever-present smell of decay radiates from the graveyard constantly.

Two things about Weselyan Cemetery make it a place fertile for ghosts: the general state of dilapidation and the traumatic death of the children at Front Street. Both things seem to have generated ghosts or at least ghost stories. The place seems to cry for help; the cemetery and the dead who inhabit it seem unable to rest.

Spring Grove Cemetery and Arboretum: The Dead Have Eyes

When one stands in Spring Grove Cemetery, there are tombs in every direction as far as the eye can see. One seems to be in a world completely different than the one outside the cemetery's

C. C. Breuer was born in 1845 in Germany and moved to Cincinnati at a very early age. He began schooling and found a great interest in the human eye. He continued to study in this field and eventually became one of the few optometrists in Cincinnati. He was able to earn a good living with this career. He lived until the age of 63, 16 years longer than the average life expectancy of the time. In 1908, he died of arteriosclerosis in Longview Hospital and was later buried in Spring Grove Cemetery. His tombstone features a bronze bust of himself with two eyes made of glass. It is in these eyes that the spirit of C. C. Breuer is said to remain. These glass eyes will sometimes follow visitors as they walk past the marker.

Gothic stone gates. Here is a world populated by the dead—populated by memories of those who lie beneath the soil.

The cemetery covers a daunting 733 acres of land, making it the second-largest cemetery in the country after Rose Hills Memorial Park in Whittier, California. Inside the towering, stone walls, though, one does not really feel the expansive size of the place. The land is hilly and dotted with clumps of trees. There are tombstones as far as one can see in any direction, but it is impossible to see more than 100 yards in any direction. It seems like an endless forest of foliage and stone.

Spring Grove Cemetery was created as the need for burial places was quickly escalating in the early 1800s. In the early 1800s, there was a huge population explosion in Cincinnati, and the municipal burial grounds within the city were becoming overcrowded. A lot of the faith-specific graveyards were expanding into the areas just outside the city, such as St. Bernard, Delhi, and Walnut Hills, but these graveyards were also filling up quickly.

Cincinnati realized that it needed a large nondenominational cemetery that was near the city to cope with the rising population. In order to fill this need, the city chartered Spring Grove Cemetery as a rural cemetery just outside the city in 1845. Near the end of August 1845, the grounds were officially consecrated, and the first burial occurred shortly thereafter.

Spring Grove became a cemetery that could cater to the burial needs of the rich and poor alike. One could purchase large plots and construct huge monuments on those plots, but the poor could also afford a sufficient burial plot in which to spend eternity. The classes of Cincinnati were able to come together in one place after death.

The cemetery began to set itself apart from other cemeteries in the area in another way. It began to focus on the landscaping and beauty of the place more so than simply arranging the burial plots. The cemetery soon became quite picturesque as the swamps were drained to make lakes. The grounds were hilly and beautiful. Artistically spaced groups of trees would offer shade to the benches, which were interspersed within the grounds. Several state champion trees have lived within Spring Grove Cemetery.

People began coming to the cemetery for reasons other than to visit loved ones. Locals were beginning to view it as a park, and people would often visit the cemetery just to take walks and enjoy the scenery. The main gate was eventually equipped with restrooms, and other shelters and facilities were spaced out throughout the grounds. Eventually Spring Grove Cemetery would change its name to Spring Grove Cemetery and Arboretum in order to express that this was more than a cemetery. These lands were a tranquil and beautiful place in which one could choose to spend a relaxing afternoon.

But despite this outward beauty that covers this immense cemetery, the grounds are still reputedly haunted by a large eclectic variety of spirits.

Perhaps the most famous ghost of Spring Grove Cemetery is the ghost of C. C. Breuer. Somewhere deep within the heart of this expansive graveyard stands a monument that marks C. C. Breuer's final resting place. It is a gray stone obelisk that towers coldly near an access road. It is marked as lot 100. Stone markers line the soil at its base, and a bronze bust sits halfway up its face.

His ghost is said to reside in this bronze bust. Legends say that the eyes in this bust will follow any passersby. His eyes will look down on anyone who dares to tread near his tomb. Some legends even claim that the eyes in the bust are the actual eyes of C. C. Breuer himself, somehow preserved and mounted within his monument.

Despite this being the most popular ghost story to come from within Spring Grove, in all likelihood, this story is only myth and exaggeration. C. C. Breuer was a rather unremarkable man in life. Interestingly enough when examined beside the legend that accompanies him, he was an optometrist in life. He spent his life helping people to see better and treating any ailments that might inflict one's eyes. Throughout his life, he became somewhat obsessed with eyes and eyesight.

Breuer was born in Germany in 1845 and moved to Cincinnati at a rather young age. In the mid-1800s, many Germans were coming into the Cincinnati area and settling there. Even today, many Cincinnatians can claim German ancestry. When Breuer moved into Cincinnati, he decided to pursue a life of study. He discovered that he was most interested in eyes and eyesight so began studying ailments of the eyes. Soon he was able to start treating some of these ailments of the eyes.

He became one of the few optometrists in Cincinnati at the time, so he was able to make a good living at it. He lived out the rest of his life in this way. He made no major strides in the fields that he studied. He died on August 20, 1908, at the age of 63. In 1908, the average life expectancy was only 47 years, so Breuer was much older when he died than most other people in the world. He died of a very common ailment as well. He died in Longview Hospital of arteriosclerosis, the hardening of the arteries of the heart. This was one of the top five leading causes of death in 1908 as well.

There were no great tragedies in his life. He did not die at an early age or of an unusual and sudden calamity. In fact, he died rather painlessly after having lived a full and satisfactory life.

So why is his ghost reputed to haunt these grounds? The answer to that probably lies within the grave marker itself. When Breuer was preparing his grave site at Spring Grove for when his day would eventually come, he wanted a marker at his grave that was unlike any other. He decided that the marker should memorialize him in a very unique way.

The marker that he chose to have constructed for him was a large stone obelisk. On the front of the obelisk were his name and a bronze bust of himself, carved in detail. Then he decided to add the final unique touch to the bronze bust of himself. Since he was an eye doctor, he had a large stock of glass eyes, many of which were so meticulously crafted that it was almost impossible to tell them from real eyes. He chose two glass eyes that were the same color as his own and had them placed within the bronze bust.

Today the marker does look incredibly eerie upon approaching it. It looks very much like there are two real eyes gazing out from the bronze bust. Sometimes, these glass eyes can even appear to follow one around as one examines the marker. Perhaps the ghost of Breuer is looking out through these glass eyes for all eternity.

Whether or not his ghost inhabits lot 100 at the cemetery, there are other reports of strange occurrences across this vast cemetery. Some other people who have been laid to rest in this cemetery do have reason to haunt these grounds throughout eternity. While there are thousands of people buried in the cemetery, a few died suddenly and unexpectedly. Some of these people even died in very strange ways. Sudden and unusual death can sometimes create ghosts.

These other stories about the cemetery are less concrete, and some people who work at the cemetery strongly assert that the cemetery is not haunted at all. The stories are stories passed from employee to employee, and the original witness to the reported occurrences has become lost. Perhaps the stories have even become embellished over the years.

Charles Franklin Mitchell's grave is supposedly one of these haunted sites. Mitchell was a politician from New York who was elected to the U.S. House of Representatives in 1836. Mitchell had worked in the milling business in Lockport, New York, before being elected to the House of Representatives. When his second term was up in 1841, he was convicted of forgery. He was sentenced to Sing Sing Prison in New York.

He was disgraced; his political career was over. He was apparently in poor health, and they felt that he would not last in the prison. He was pardoned and was able to avoid imprisonment. In disgrace, Mitchell moved to Ohio where he lived out the rest of his years in anonymity.

When he died in 1865, he was buried in Spring Grove Cemetery. His grave is in section 87, lot 20, and it is a simple family stone. The name Mitchell is etched on a large central marker while the individual graves are on the ground in front of the marker.

Some people report having seen ghostly white dogs that tend to congregate near Mitchell's grave site. The dogs appear almost spectral and have glowing eyes. Legends say that if one ever encounters these ghostly dogs, one will be afflicted by a streak of bad luck. Perhaps this is due to Mitchell's own rotten luck in life. Perhaps these ghostly dogs are somehow remnants of Mitchell's anger and shame at his loss of station in life. Their strange power to imbue their witnesses with bad luck could just be Mitchell, cursing others as he himself was cursed in life.

Other stories from Spring Grove Cemetery will often simply involve ghostly figures seen walking through the cemetery and then vanishing into the night. These shadowy figures will often wander aimlessly and then simply vanish, or they will walk to a headstone and sit down and rest against it only to vanish into the shadows.

Are these figures just tricks of the shadows and the light, or are they the ghosts of some of those tragic deaths that occurred to some of the dead here at Spring Grove?

In 1884, a man named William Berner convinced his coworker to help him rob their boss. Their boss was a stableman named William Kirk who owned a stable on West Eighth Street near Mound Street. Despite the fact that he only had a small sum of money, Berner and his coworker Joseph Palmer brutally attacked Kirk in order to get the money. They beat Kirk until he was unconscious on the floor, and then they strangled him until he was dead.

Immediately afraid of the consequences of their actions, they decided that they would hide the body so that no one could be sure that he was dead. They tossed the body into a wagon and took it to the outskirts of town. They hid the body in a thicket and went back to the city, thinking that no one would be the wiser.

They were caught and sent to trial. The mentality of the time was that murderers deserved to die, and Palmer was hung for the brutal murder. Berner, on the other hand, was able to secure a good defense lawyer who was able to get Berner off with only 20 years in prison.

The town was furious, and the verdict resulted in the bloodiest riot in the history of Cincinnati, the Cincinnati Courthouse Riot of 1884. There would be about 56 deaths before the rioting ended. Berner would survive and spend the next 20 years in prison. Kirk's body would eventually be discovered. He is buried in section 16 at Spring Grove Cemetery. Perhaps his ghost is one of these shadows that still walk the night at the cemetery.

Another tragedy occurred in 1889 when six people were killed in an accident at Mount Auburn. In the late 1800s, the city was growing quickly and people wanted to begin settling in the outlying hills of Cincinnati. The hills were far too steep to make travel to the city easy for anyone who lived up there, so the city decided to build a series of mechanical inclines to aid in the growth of the city.

These inclines were mechanical vehicles that were pulled up and lowered down these steep hills. Citizens who lived at the top of these hills could easily just take these inclines into the city and not have to take long winding roads to go down the hills.

These inclines operated safely until 1889, when the accident occurred. As the car started lowering its seven riders to the bottom of the Mount Auburn incline, the cable snapped. At the complete mercy of gravity, the car raced down the hill and broke through the bottom of the incline. The roof of the incline car was torn off as it slammed into some nearby buildings on Mulberry Street. Only one of the riders in the car survived the accident.

At least one of the passengers who were killed in the accident, a judge from Cincinnati, was buried in Spring Grove Cemetery. Perhaps his sudden, unusual, and unexpected death has caused his spirit to forever wander Spring Grove as a shadowy presence in the night.

A man named Isaac Jordan is also buried in the cemetery near the famous graves of Salmon P. Chase, the chief justice of the Supreme Court, and Joseph Hooker, the Civil War general. Jordan was a politician from his college days. He actually founded the Sigma Chi fraternity in 1855.

A few years later he would be elected as a Democrat to the U.S. House of Representatives. He served from 1883 until 1885. His life would also end in a tragic accident though.

In 1890, he was riding an elevator in a building in downtown Cincinnati when the cable suddenly broke. In 1890, basic elevator safety features had not yet been invented, so the elevator car that was carrying Jordan plummeted to the bottom of the shaft, killing all who were on board. Perhaps Jordan still walks the grounds at night, a victim of unusual and unexpected circumstances.

A groundskeeper would later tell a chilling story of what happened to him as he walked by a man named Charlie Grant's grave in Spring Grove Cemetery.

In life, Charlie Grant was a baseball player. He was an African American player in the early 1900s, so he was unable to play in the major leagues due to the racism of the time. He played in the Negro League, and he was a very good player.

A man named John McGraw of the Baltimore Orioles saw him play and knew that he would be an asset to their major-league team. Since it was against the rules to have an African American on the team, they decided to disguise Grant as a Native American instead. In 1901, Charlie Grant joined an American League baseball team under the pseudonym Charlie Tokohama.

In the first game that Grant was going to play against the Chicago White Sox, the president of the White Sox objected, arguing that Grant was actually an African American. Grant stuck to the story, claiming that his mother was from Kansas and that his father was a Cherokee Indian. He was allowed to stay on the team, but since their trick had been discovered, Grant was kept on the bench throughout the game. The Orioles did not want anyone to do any official investigations.

Eventually, Grant was forced out of the Orioles and went back to playing in the Negro League. Since he could not pay the bills with the money he made in the Negro League, Grant had to work other odd jobs in order to make ends meet.

In 1932, he was working as the doorman for an apartment building in Cincinnati. While he was sitting on the front doorsteps of the apartment building, a car that was passing on the road blew a tire. It careened out of control and slammed into Grant, killing him.

A groundskeeper was walking through section 53 where Grant is buried when suddenly he felt a hand grab him by the ankle. He panicked and tried to run, but the hand held him tightly. Eventually he was able to pull free and run away. He refused to go back to see what had happened. The other employees who he told his story to went back to the spot and saw no evidence that the ground had been upset in any way.

Did the groundskeeper catch his pant leg on something so that it felt like someone had grabbed his ankle, or had the ghost of Charlie Grant, still here in this world after the unexpected accident and frustrating career, reached up from his grave to grab the passing groundskeeper?

Spring Grove Cemetery is a peaceful home for the dead. In a vast graveyard such as this, without another living soul for as far as the eye can see, light and dark can play a lot of tricks on those who are there to observe them. The living are only visitors, subject to the watchful eyes of the true residents of these grounds.

Ten

SCHOOL AND PLAY

Everything has the potential to have a dark side, even those things that seem to encourage nothing but joy and amusement, perhaps especially those things that were meant to encourage joy. When the darker side of these things comes into the forefront, it is more unexpected. A merry-go-round is meant as a ride on which to have fun, but what happens when the mechanisms inside break down and helpless riders are thrown to the ground. A swimming pool is meant as a relaxing place to spend a warm day, but what happens when one cannot swim. A park is meant as a place to rest, relax, and have fun, but what happens when the ghosts who reside there are not at rest and they have forgotten how to have fun.

The Cincinnati Zoo: Stalked by a Lioness

Who says that ghosts have to have once been human? From time to time supernatural stories will surface where the entities seem to have nothing to do with humanity. Phantom dogs seem to be the most common. Haunted places will often have stories where dogs will seem to congregate around certain areas. These dogs will often either inexplicably vanish or will scare off those unlucky enough to witness them.

Vampires, witches, and Satanists, staples of any scary story, will often have animals associated with them as some kind of henchmen, as some kind of creature that harbors the same powers as these classic scary figures. Black cats and vampire bats are likely to instigate fear and discomfort to those who encounter them in the night.

But even through all these instances of animals appearing in ghost stories, their ghosts are intrinsically different than those ghosts of human beings. In these classic ghost tales involving animals, the animals are associated with humanlike creatures, or they signify bad omens or guardians of the sacred places they haunt.

The ghost who inhabits the Cincinnati Zoo is somewhat different than these classic examples of animal ghosts. Here the famous ghost of the lioness that walks these asphalt paths does not seem to realize that she is dead. She takes on the attributes of a human ghost and continues to act in the way that she would have had she never died. While most animals associated with ghosts seem to have otherworldly motives or are controlled by other sentient beings, the lioness of the Cincinnati Zoo continues to behave by the same instincts she exhibited in life. Her hunting ground is the historic and world-famous Cincinnati Zoo itself.

Few people know that the Cincinnati Zoo was most probably the result of an attack on the city by caterpillars. In 1872, huge numbers of caterpillars descended on Cincinnati and were quickly eating all the city's vegetation. A group of prominent Cincinnatians decided that they were going to solve this problem. They formed the Society for the Acclimatization of Birds. They purchased 1,000 birds from Europe and housed them in a big building in the city. Then they released the birds upon the caterpillar plague that had infested the city.

The plan worked, and the caterpillar population decreased significantly. The Society for the Acclimatization of Birds changed its name to the Cincinnati Zoological Society and decided to open up a zoo. The Cincinnati Zoo opened in 1875 as the Cincinnati Zoological Gardens. It was the second zoo to open in the entire country. It opened only a year and two months after

This building was constructed in 1875 and is the oldest zoo building in the western hemisphere. A local architect named James McLaughlin designed this building along with many of the original buildings in the zoo. Originally this building held primates. This continued until 1951, when the building was converted into the reptile house. The reptile house is one of the many structures here at the zoo that have been designated national historic landmarks. The elephant house and the passenger pigeon memorial buildings also share the distinction of being named national historic landmarks. Today the zoo is one of the largest and most highly regarded zoos in the world. It houses more than 500 different animal species and more than 3,000 different plant species. According to legend, the zoo is haunted by a lioness who stalks hapless visitors throughout the zoo.

the Philadelphia Zoo, which opened in July 1874. The reptile house in the Cincinnati Zoo still stands today and is the oldest zoo building in the western hemisphere.

Originally the zoo only had a small allotment of animals within its grounds. It had eight monkeys, six raccoons, three deer, two elk, a buffalo, a hyena, a tiger, an alligator, and many birds. The zoo also had a circus elephant in its collection that was a favorite of early visitors.

The zoo would grow over the years and become one of the greatest zoos in the entire world. It is renowned for its breeding program and is known for its educational programs.

Many years of history have occurred within these grounds. Many different animals have been removed from their natural habitat to be brought here and studied and saved from the brink of extinction.

Even this renowned zoo could not save some species from extinction. Martha, the world's final passenger pigeon, was housed at this zoo. As the final specimen, the bird was unable to breed. With the continuation of its species ultimately hopeless, it died alone at the Cincinnati Zoo, forever passing into extinction.

The lioness who haunts these grounds is perhaps a remnant of the rich history of this place. No one knows which lion from the history of this place is the one whose spirit hunts these grounds. Many lions have passed away throughout the years at the zoo, but none have done so in an overly traumatic way. Perhaps her spirit was just too strong to simply fade away, and it lives on, haunting these grounds.

Strangely, the lioness does not haunt a certain section of the zoo, nor is there a certain time of the day or night where experiences involving this ghost happen. The zoo as a whole seems to be uniformly haunted by this entity.

The stories about this lioness are similar every time that they are reported. Once a visitor to the zoo separated from his family and decided to walk the grounds alone for a while. As he was walking down a wooded path alone, he heard soft footsteps behind him. He glanced over his shoulder but saw that there was nothing there. He began to walk again, and the footsteps followed. The man stopped again, and the footsteps stopped. He was beginning to become concerned because he was certain that he was hearing the footsteps, and the footsteps did not sound like echoes or like his own footsteps at all. He thought that it sounded like a large animal following him through the path. The man began to quicken his pace in an effort to escape whatever was following him, but the footsteps quickened their pace as well.

Eventually the man broke into a run and heard a growl that sounded like a lion behind him. Now he was sure that a lion had escaped and was chasing him down the trail. He ran as fast as he could in an attempt to reach the safety of a large group of people. Listening to the footsteps, though, he realized that he was not going to make it; the lion would be on top of him long before he reached safety. Just as the footsteps and the growling were upon him, he turned to face his attacker.

There was nothing there. The footsteps had stopped. The growling had stopped. The man began to wonder if he had actually experienced the chase.

This was not an isolated experience. Oftentimes people will feel as if they have been involved in a similar chase. Those who experience it almost always report hearing soft footsteps, like those of a lion, following them down lonely paths of the zoo. When these people turn around upon hearing the footsteps, there is nothing there behind them, but as soon as they begin walking again, the footsteps resume. If these witnesses quicken their pace in an attempt to escape this invisible stalker, the pace of the phantom footsteps will quicken in turn. Growls will often accompany the footsteps in these stories. The attacks always end the same way though; just when the victim thinks that the lion is on top of them, they will turn around and there is nothing there. Sometimes the hunted will reach another group of people before the lion is upon them, and in this case the chase will stop as well. The lion will only hunt victims when they are walking alone.

Other stories about the zoo involve mysterious glowing green eyes that will sometimes materialize in the wooded sections of the zoo or at the end of dark hallways in buildings. These green eyes will seem to watch those witnessing them until those witnesses reach a more populated place, and these eyes will oftentimes accompany the phantom footsteps and growling that people frequently encounter.

The zoo itself is a beautiful expanse of property. Many varieties of animal and plant life are interwoven throughout this world-famous zoo. Moving from one path to another, one will oftentimes feel as if one has left the Midwest and entered an entirely different part of the world.

This place, this home for so many animals over so many years, is guarded though. A sentinel, a lioness long dead, will stalk those who happen to wander off by themselves. She continues to hunt like she had in life.

Coney Island: Carnival of Souls

At night, Coney Island can be a scary place. It is no longer the scene of children's laughter. It is no longer a place where people come to spend a day with the rides and attractions that whirl and rise constantly during the park's hours of operation. It is an abandoned place. It is a scary place where ghosts of its past come to haunt the grounds.

At night, it is said that one can hear the distant chants of Native Americans. Perhaps these ghostly chants are paranormal echoes from when this area housed ancient Native American tribes. Coney Island is not far from Woodland Mound, an ancient Native American burial site. These disembodied chants seem to come from all around as one stands within the grounds of Coney Island at night.

On clear nights, mysterious fogs settle over the Coney Island area. The fogs have no earthly explanation, but again they work to add to the already scary ambiance of the place. Perhaps fogs from another world settle over the park to allow those who have passed on to enjoy the haunted amusement park in the abandoned nighttime air. Spirits can play at night in the cover of fog without having to worry about any worldly interference.

Screams are also often heard echoing through the park at night. The screams themselves seem to be focused around several specific rides. They are most clearly heard near the carousel and the Scrambler rides. It is as if the ghosts want passersby to hear their ghostly screams at these specific locations.

Water at Sunlite Pool, the largest filtered pool in the world, seems to splash with no discernable source. It is almost as if there is someone playing out in the middle of the pool, but no animals or people are there.

Perhaps the creepiest place to venture at night is Moonlight Gardens. A man named George Schott constructed Moonlight Gardens in 1925 as an open-air dance hall. It was immediately a hit and became the recreational center of the park until the present day. Today, though, it is haunted by the ghost of Schott, who died unexpectedly at Moonlight Gardens of a heart attack.

Once an employee was roaming through Moonlight Gardens at night, making one last sweep of the place before they locked the area up for the night. As she crossed the floor on her way to the exit, she felt a chill crawl down her spine and felt as if she was being watched. She spun around and looked all around her but was unable to see anyone until she looked up to the balcony. Up on the balcony she saw a man standing there quietly watching her.

She immediately fled and found another employee to whom she reported the trespasser. They both went back and searched the balcony for the man. No one was there, and all the entrances to get up there had been locked up and blocked off. No one could have been up there without a key.

Many times people will report a male figure in early-1900s clothing looking down from the second floor of Moonlight Gardens to the dance floor below. Sometimes he is reported to be standing next to a ghostly woman. People who see him are immediately filled with a deep sense of dread. Perhaps this ominous spirit is George Schott, who died in this very section of the park. This spirit seems to want people, trespassers or not, to leave its beloved Moonlight Gardens.

During the day, Coney Island is masked by the guise of an amusement park—a place to bring the family to have fun. At night, though, the true side of Coney Island comes out, the darker side, the demons and the ghosts warning those unlucky enough to walk these streets at night that the living are no longer welcome here. The eerie fog will from time to time descend into this place, perhaps for no other reason than to remind the living that they are not welcome here once the sun goes down.

What kind of dark history could have spawned the eerie ambience that surrounds this place? By the early 1800s, the European settlers had driven the Native Americans who had once hunted and cultivated this land farther west. Countless years of prosperity had been interrupted by unwelcome invaders from the east. Perhaps the spirits of those Native Americans who were unwilling to abandon their lands still chant long into the night.

The Coney Island grounds remained mostly untouched despite being only 10 miles east of the city of Cincinnati until 1867, when a man named James Parker purchased these 40 acres of land. Since the land sat on the shore of the Ohio River, the soil was fertile and Parker was able to cultivate an apple orchard on his land.

Over the next few years, several travelers passing by Parker's land would ask him if they could set up a picnic there. The land was beautiful. Glistening waters flowed to the south. Trees and nature were all around, creating a virtual Eden, the perfect place to relax and have a picnic.

Travelers stopped by so often that Parker began making a business out of it. He would rent out the land to travelers wanting to picnic or hold small events on his land. Soon he would make enough money at this that he was able to build a dance hall, a dining hall, and a mule-powered carousel.

It became so successful that a business known as the Ohio Grove Corporation purchased the land from Parker in 1886 so that it could set up an official amusement park and take advantage of the site. It added rides to the park and purchased a steamboat that would carry parkgoers from the nearby metropolis of Cincinnati to the park. It dubbed the park "the Coney Island of the West" after the famous amusement park in New York. The name caught on and was eventually shortened to simply Coney Island.

Every year the owners would add new rides, and the park became the most popular amusement park in this part of the country. Eventually, though, the park would fall on hard times. Another amusement park was built closer to Cincinnati. Patrons could go to the other amusement park by streetcar instead of having to ride the steamboat upriver. Also, being so close to the river, any floods would virtually wipe out the park. Up into the early 1900s, several floods destroyed the park to the point where it nearly went out of business.

Another huge blow came when the stock market crashed in 1929. Few people could afford such frivolous things as amusement parks so Coney Island's patronage went way down. Again it nearly closed, but somehow it was able to survive the Great Depression and pull through stronger on the other side. By this time, George Schott was the owner of the park, and he was able to keep it afloat despite the hard times.

By the end of the Great Depression, Coney Island was the only amusement park in the area that had not gone out of business. After World War II, better roads were built that made it easier to get to the park. In the latter half of the 20th century, Coney Island grew into the park that it is today.

But that does not mean that everything that happened as the park flourished was a positive thing. Beyond the tragic death of George Schott in 1935, several other tragedies have occurred on these grounds.

James Parker purchased this property in 1867. At that time, it was nothing more than a large apple orchard. Over the years, people would ask to camp on Parker's land or picnic there, and Parker would welcome them. As more and more visitors would stop by, Parker began to rent the land to those who wanted to use it. Eventually he decided to set up a small amusement park. The park was so popular that the Ohio Grove Corporation bought the park in 1886. When people came to the park, they would come over on this ferry known as the Island Queen. Since there were no good roads that came out this far from Cincinnati at the time, patrons would ride the ferry to the park and home at the end of the day. The Ohio Grove Corporation continued to add rides and attractions, and the park became known as "the Coney Island of the West." As time went by and streetcars became more common, patrons no longer needed the ferry, and it went out of service.

Sunlite Pool is the largest recirculating pool in the world. This enormous pool stretches over 200 feet wide and 401 feet in length. The shallow end is a mere 6 inches deep, and the deep end descends 10½ feet. It requires more than 3.5 million gallons of water to fill the pool during the warm summer months. A pool this size requires an enormous filtration system. The filtration system is large enough to meet the needs of a city with a population exceeding 200,000. Not surprisingly, a pool with such a long history has seen a lot of patrons. Most of them live to tell about their adventures in the pool; however, Earl T. Gilpin was not so fortunate. He died in the pool in 1944. Legend says he still walks the grounds at night.

On August 6, 1949, there was an incident at the carousel in the park. A 68-year-old widow had attended the park with her family. She initially had no inclination to ride the merry-go-round, but a family member convinced her to do so. She mounted one of the plaster horses and nervously held on as the ride moved up and down as it turned slowly around. Halfway through the ride she was struck with a dizzy spell. She held on throughout the remainder of the ride, but when the ride stopped, she toppled to the ground, suffering a fractured skull. Despite help arriving immediately, she lapsed into unconsciousness on the way to the ambulance. Thirty minutes later she died at Christ Hospital.

Another fatality occurred at the Scrambler ride several years later. A nine-year-old boy named Russell Mack Jr. rode the ride with his aunt while his parents watched their brother-in-law's children. Suddenly the door flew open. His aunt was able to grab the other two kids who rode with them, but Russell was already gone. Russell fell from the spinning car, and before the controller of the ride could do anything, another spinning car smashed into the hapless boy. Emergency crews rushed Russell to the hospital immediately with a fractured skull and internal hemorrhaging. He died three hours later in Christ Hospital. Looking back at the tragedy, Russell's aunt could not figure out what had caused the door to come swinging open. The president of Coney Island assumed that the boy had been messing with the latch and had somehow managed to undo it.

On Sunday May 28, 1944, Earl T. Gilpin, a 32-year-old father was swimming in Sunlite Pool with several friends. The group of friends decided they would try to swim to the middle of the pool where a small island floats in the water. Gilpin dove off a low diving board, and he and his friends raced to the island. When the friends reached the island at the center of the pool, they noticed Gilpin was missing. The lifeguards saw him at the bottom of the 10-foot section and rushed to attempt to save him. They pulled him from the water and attempted to revive him for 40 minutes before he was pronounced dead. After the incident, witnesses noticed that his face had been badly bruised and there was a gash near his eye. He had probably hit the bottom of the pool when he jumped in. If the impact had not killed him, his weak heart probably had. He was being treated for heart problems, so a sudden heart attack could also have led to the fatality.

Coney Island also used to host automobile races. One of these automobile races also ended in tragedy. Thirty-three-year-old Earl Calvin was driving when his steering gear suddenly locked. He went through a barrier and slammed into a wall. He was taken from the car with several broken ribs, a broken shoulder, and a punctured lung. Emergency crews rushed him to the hospital where they performed an operation in an attempt to save his life, but their efforts failed. He died later that evening.

Earlier that same race, a driver named Al Thiesen lost control of his vehicle and slid through a fence. Once at a stop, his vehicle burst into flames, seriously burning him. By the time any of the spectators could arrive to save him from the fire, he was badly burned and bruised. He was rushed to the hospital and fortunately was saved from any permanent injury.

Coney Island began as a simple park where people could bring their picnics. From there it evolved to the amusement park that sits at the site today. People used to take steamboats to get to the park; now they drive there. The park has been redone several times since it was built in 1886, be it to repair damage done by rising floodwaters or just to keep the park fun and up-to-date.

But despite how much has changed, how similar or different the park looks than it did back in 1886, the angry spirits of those souls who have perished on these grounds through the years continue to inhabit Coney Island after dark.

Haunted High Schools

Certain sounds will repeat like a broken record in a high school. Lockers slam; voices will speak about day-to-day occurrences; books will drop and close; teachers' voices will drone on and on; doors will slam, their latches catching hollowly; footsteps will sound, echoing down the hallways, hiding their tangible source; wind will blow through cracked windows and through cracked doors.

As the doors lock for the evening, classes having long since let out, the wind still blows. The lockers are still there, filled with books. But since the people have left the building vacant for the evening the footsteps are much more difficult to hear.

Anderson High School

The stories that have surfaced about the school's resident ghosts are repeated time after time, even by those who had not heard the legends before. The witnesses who experience these ghosts are always the night janitors who inhabit the building long after the students and faculty have left for the evening.

Anderson is set up much like any other high school. Its halls stretch down the length of the building, lined with lockers, punctuated by evenly spaced classroom doors. Since the building opened in 1964, many additions have changed the shape of the building. Today, if the school is looked at from the air, it would resemble the letter A. The history of the building is by no means long, nor is it marred by any dark stories that might be used in some sort of ghost tale. No murders or suicides have occurred on the school's campus; no accidents or even deaths seem to have occurred on these grounds.

The school's ghosts are never seen. Two basic accounts of the ghosts' activities are all that exist in reference to the Anderson High School spirits. The first account is told by the janitors who work in the school after hours. Once a couple of janitors were cleaning up the school in the later hours of the evening. It was well after school hours, so the building was empty. The teachers, students, and administration had all left long ago for the night. As the janitors were cleaning up some of the garbage that had been left in one of the lower levels of the school, they began to hear voices that sounded like students coming from somewhere in the building.

The janitors were so sure that they had heard these children's voices that they decided that they had to search the building and find these trespassers. They soon found that this was not as easy as it originally seemed. They could not discover where the voices were coming from. They would hear the voices coming from all around them. The janitors searched the building for more than an hour for the source of these voices. They were never able to find anyone else in the building.

This same story is told time and again by the night janitors at Anderson High School. Oftentimes they will stop their work to go looking for the children in the building, but they are never able to find anyone.

The second account of the ghosts of Anderson High School is told by students who come in for their morning classes. These students will report that some of their belongings that they left in certain rooms in the school are missing. They look everywhere throughout that room for the items that they are sure that they left there. But it is to no avail; the items are missing. Later on, though, it is discovered that their belongings are not missing but have been moved to an entirely different room in the school building. The students clearly remember leaving these items in one place, but somehow these items end up in an entirely different and unlikely location. If this were to happen once, it could be easily explained away as faulty memory on the part of the student, but this strange occurrence has been reported to have happened many different times in the school's history.

Perhaps the midnight voices can be explained away as a trick of the wind blowing down the long empty hallways. But if that were the case, why would the janitors waste their time investigating the whole building? Perhaps the displacement of the students' belongings can be explained as someone else mistaking the belongings as their own and moving them to a different room or a weak recollection on the part of the victim. But if that were the case, why is the phenomenon reported so frequently?

Mother of Mercy High School

Mother of Mercy High School was founded in 1915 as a school that catered to girls of all ages, from grades 1 to 12. Most of the building that stands there in Westwood on Werk Road was built in 1923. By 1977, the school only accommodated grades 9 to 12, and today it is considered one of the best high schools in the Cincinnati area.

But the building is haunted. Almost all the students know about the ghost of Mother of Mercy High School. Those in the theater department actually have a name for the ghost. They call her Sr. Mary Carlos, the namesake of the auditorium in the school where the theater department performs.

The students and faculty involved in the theater department follow a very strange tradition when preparing themselves for a show. On the night before the final dress rehearsal, it is tradition for the director and the stage manager to stay after everyone else has left and invite their resident ghost, Sr. Mary Carlos, to the opening-night performance. Apparently this ceremony is taken quite seriously and even sometimes involves candles to make the ceremony seem more official. They hold this ceremony inviting their ghost to the play because, as the stories go, if they do not, Sr. Mary Carlos will come to opening night and wreak havoc with the performance.

Most of the stories that are associated with Sr. Mary Carlos occur during opening night at one of the school's plays. Oftentimes the lights will flicker for no apparent reason, and props will be moved around and lost. This only seems to happen during those performances where Sr. Mary Carlos is not invited to the opening-night performance.

There is a story about this happening rather recently. Only a few years ago, everything was so busy with the theater show that the director forgot to invite the ghost to the opening-night performance of the show. While everything was fine in dress rehearsals, as soon as the actual show started, things started going terribly wrong.

The crew has to use walkie-talkies in order to communicate and make sure that all scene transitions go smoothly. On this particular night, the walkie-talkies would not work properly. There was only static and broken words that came through any of the walkie-talkies, so they were completely worthless. The heads of all the different departments had to run all around in order to establish any semblance of order between the departments.

On the same night, something was happening in the prop department. All the props had been moved around. The girl in charge of the props could not find a lot of the stuff that she had so carefully set up the night before. It was as if someone had come in and hidden the important things that she needed and had rearranged everything so that the play could not run smoothly.

Once the performance was over, the director realized that all the problems that occurred during the opening-night performance were probably due to Sr. Mary Carlos. With profuse apologies, the director invited the ghost to the next evening's performance.

The next night, the performance went off flawlessly. Not a single thing went wrong.

Mount Notre Dame High School

Mount Notre Dame is one of the older schools in the Cincinnati area. It actually dates back to before the Civil War. It opened as a boarding school on September 17, 1860. The school was exclusively for women, and girls from all around the country came here in order to learn. Two of Civil War general William T. Sherman's daughters actually came to this school in order to learn.

With its great reputation, the school quickly flourished and expanded. Students no longer were forced to board at the school in 1897, and boys were first admitted in 1929. By 1935, the

Mother of Mercy High School was built in 1923 on Werk Road in Westwood. Originally it was meant to be a secondary school for area women, but the needs of the area dictated that the school be used as both an elementary and secondary school for young women. It would continue to house an elementary school for a number of years before becoming the exclusively secondary school that it is today. This is the front entrance to the main building of the school. This section houses the haunted auditorium. In 1943, another wing was added. Since then, two more sections have been added onto the school. One section, built in 1965, houses the gymnasium and nine additional classrooms, and another section, finished in 2007, houses the technical section of the school with three computer labs.

boarding school closed down, leaving a school that taught all grades from kindergarten through 12th grade. It became an all-girl high school in 1956.

Despite this rich and prestigious history, there are rumors that float around that this school is haunted.

In the early 1940s, a girl at the school killed herself on the third floor of the building. The ghostly occurrences here at Mount Notre Dame High School seem to all be confined to the third floor of the building. The hauntings all seem to occur during nighttime hours, once the building has been locked up for the night.

Sometimes students will come into the building in the morning and find that all the lockers on the third floor have somehow opened by themselves. Also, sometimes the ghost will turn on every light on the third floor of the building. All the lights are turned off before the building is locked up and left for the night, but when the building is opened the next morning, the lights on the third floor, and only the lights on the third floor, have all been turned on.

Perhaps these instances are all the work of the girl who committed suicide on that floor in the 1940s. Perhaps it is all her desperate plea for recognition.

Oak Hills High School

Oak Hills High School is a public school in Green Township on the west side of Cincinnati. It sits on Ebenezer Road and is one of the best public high schools in the city.

There are rumors that Oak Hills High School has its own ghost. This ghost tends to haunt the auditorium where the school plays are performed. Those who have seen this ghost report that she is a very short but older woman. She is seen all throughout the auditorium area.

Once a faculty member saw the short woman walking around the stage. Since the teacher did not recognize her, she decided to approach the woman to see who she was and why she was on the stage. As the teacher approached the stage, she talked to the short woman, asking her who she was, but the woman on the stage did not seem to hear her. When the teacher finally stepped up onto the stage, the woman walked back behind the stage and disappeared into the backstage area. The teacher followed closely behind her, but when she got to the area backstage where she had seen the woman go, there was no one there. Other people have seen this short woman walking around in the backstage area of the auditorium or on the catwalks above the stage as well.

Other ghostly occurrences that occur in the auditorium area have been attributed to this short woman that people have reported seeing in the area. Sometimes all the lights in the auditorium will suddenly go off, even though there is no one standing near the light switches when it happens. Other times, open doors in the auditorium will inexplicably slam shut.

While luckily this ghost never seems to disturb actual performances, she is still a ghostly presence who sends chills down the spines of those who have seen her. Many thespians believe that it is good luck to perform in a haunted theater. When watching a play at Oak Hills High School, perhaps it would be worth it to scan the crowd quickly, looking for an unusually short woman. Perhaps she does not disturb the performances since she is too busy watching them.

St. Xavier High School

St. Xavier High School is the oldest high school in the city of Cincinnati and one of the oldest high schools in the entire country. It was founded in 1831 and was originally in downtown Cincinnati on Sycamore near Seventh Street, where the St. Xavier Cathedral stands today. A week later Woodward High School opened, becoming the city's first public high school.

St. Xavier thrived during the first 20 years of its existence but then was almost forced to close when the cholera epidemic of 1850 hit the city. Since people from the city were often scared of gathering within the city out of fear of cholera, enrollment at the high school fell dramatically.

The school was able to pull through the tragedy, though, and remained at its original location until 1955, when the Jesuits who ran the school purchased land in Finneytown, a small town just north of Cincinnati. The school still sits at this location in Finneytown to this day.

The ghost of St. Xavier High School is reputed to be that of a former janitor of the Finneytown building. The stories say that this janitor hung himself in a stall in one of the men's bathrooms.

Every once in a while a student or faculty member will see the ghost of this janitor within the walls of the school. Many times, students or teachers will see a janitor walking down an empty hallway. Then suddenly the janitor will stop, make eye contact with the witness, and then vanish into thin air.

Once a student was in one of the building's restrooms. It was early in the morning. The first class of the day was still almost an hour away, and only a handful of students and faculty were already in the building at this time. When the student walked into the restroom, a janitor appeared to be working on a toilet in one of the stalls. The door to the stall was open, so the student was able to clearly see the janitor. When the student went to the sinks to wash his hands, he looked at the janitor in the mirror. The janitor turned and looked back into the mirror at the student and then vanished. Startled, the student turned around to see that the door to the stall was closed and there was no one else in the restroom.

Taylor High School

Taylor was founded in 1926 in North Bend. According to rumors, two ghosts haunt this 80-year-old school building. The first ghost is that of a janitor who died here while working one day. The janitor was working on a ladder in the small room that sits just in between the two science laboratories. He was working after hours when all the students and faculty had left for the night so that he would not interfere with any classes. At some point during the evening, he had a heart attack while he was up on the ladder. This heart attack caused a nasty fall from the ladder that resulted in his death.

It was not until a secretary entered the building the next morning that the janitor's body was found. A lot of the hauntings that occur at the Taylor High School building are attributed to the ghost of this custodian.

Almost all these occurrences involve the classroom doors. Many times, during classes at the school the door to the rooms will swing open or slam closed for no reason. It happens often in the school and will disrupt classes when it happens as everyone in the room can clearly see that the door opened or closed of its own accord.

Once there was a small crew of custodians working overnight at the school. After they finished cleaning the classrooms, they would close the doors to remind themselves that that particular room was finished. When they were almost finished with the building, they noticed that a couple of the doors of the rooms that they had just cleaned were standing open. They went back through the building, checking all the doors that they were certain that they had closed. They found that every classroom door in the entire building was open. Not only this, but every door seemed to be opened at a perfect 90-degree angle.

The other ghost of Taylor High School frequents the swimming pool area at the school. The story behind this one is that a boy at the school was talking on a cell phone and somehow tripped and fell into the pool. He did not know how to swim, and his heavy clothing helped to drag him down to the pool's bottom. By the time anyone found him, he had already drowned in the pool.

Many times, in the boys' locker room adjacent to the pool, the toilets will somehow flush by themselves. Also people near the swimming pool area will hear frantic splashing coming from the pool, but when they go to check what is going on, the pool is empty and calm.

Originally St. Xavier High School was located in downtown Cincinnati on Sycamore Street between Sixth and Seventh Streets. It was built in 1831 and is the oldest high school in Cincinnati—one of the oldest high schools in the country. The school did quite well after it opened, but after low enrollment resulting from the cholera epidemic of 1850, the school nearly went out of business. Eventually the school was able to pull through the tragedy. In 1955, the school moved north to the suburbs of Cincinnati at Finneytown. Legends say that a janitor hung himself in a men's bathroom stall in this building. His ghost is sometimes seen in the bathrooms or roaming the halls to this day.

Construction on Western Hills High School started on March 27, 1926. After only two years of building, the school opened on September 11, 1928. The building was created using Renaissance architectural inspiration, and it has changed very little on the outside since it was originally built more than 75 years ago. The need for a public high school on the west side of Cincinnati was the driving force behind this school's creation. The city purchased 28½ acres of land for $43,860 on which to build the school. The school building itself cost $1,145,000 to complete. The ghost of this school haunts the now-defunct swimming pool area near the gymnasium and the locker rooms.

Western Hills High School

Western Hills High School is on Ferguson Road near the Price Hill region of Cincinnati and is part of the Cincinnati Public School district. The ghost stories that come out of this building are kind of strange, and there does not seem to be a historical reason for these hauntings.

The doors that sit between the boys' and girls' locker rooms lead to what used to be the school's swimming pool. Today the pool is empty, but the area in which this empty pool sits is where the hauntings of West High supposedly take place.

The story goes that back in the days when the pool was still in use there was a foreign exchange student who decided that he wanted to skip out of classes and use the pool. Since there was not anyone who was using the pool during this particular period, he figured he could relax and have the entire pool to himself.

When he walked into the room with the pool, it was very dark. He could hardly see a thing. Suddenly a loud noise came from behind him. Frightened, he ran away from the sound but ended up tripping and falling into the swimming pool. This was at 1:24 p.m.

A janitor, who was working nearby, heard the screaming and splashing coming from the pool, so he switched on the lights and rushed into the room. He saw the student in the pool splashing around. It seemed like he was being wrestled and pulled under the water. Finally the janitor was able to save the boy, but the area has retained its reputation for being haunted.

It seems that the time of day has some significance to the haunting. Oftentimes, if someone is in the pool area at 1:24 p.m. they can hear screams and splashing coming from the pool. When those who hear these sounds go and check, the pool area is always empty. Even now that the pool is no longer in use and there is no water in the pool, people will still hear the screams and splashing coming from the pool area near 1:24 in the afternoon.

DISCOVER THOUSANDS OF LOCAL HISTORY BOOKS
FEATURING MILLIONS OF VINTAGE IMAGES

Arcadia Publishing, the leading local history publisher in the United States, is committed to making history accessible and meaningful through publishing books that celebrate and preserve the heritage of America's people and places.

Find more books like this at
www.arcadiapublishing.com

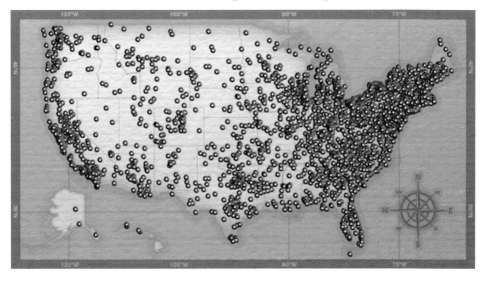

Search for your hometown history, your old stomping grounds, and even your favorite sports team.

Consistent with our mission to preserve history on a local level, this book was printed in South Carolina on American-made paper and manufactured entirely in the United States. Products carrying the accredited Forest Stewardship Council (FSC) label are printed on 100 percent FSC-certified paper.

MADE IN THE

3 1333 04483 9007